Welfare

Other Books of Related Interest:

At Issue Series

Are America's Wealthy Too Powerful?
Child Labor and Sweatshops
How Can the Poor Be Helped?

Current Controversies Series

Jobs in America

Introducing Issues with Opposing Viewpoints Series

The U.S. Economy

Issues That Concern You Series

Teens and Employment

"Congress shall make no law ... abridging the freedom of speech, or of the press."

First Amendment to the US Constitution

The basic foundation of our democracy is the First Amendment guarantee of freedom of expression. The *Opposing Viewpoints* Series is dedicated to the concept of this basic freedom and the idea that it is more important to practice it than to enshrine it.

OPPOSING VIEWPOINTS® SERIES

Welfare

Margaret Haerens, Book Editor

GREENHAVEN PRESS
A part of Gale, Cengage Learning

GALE
CENGAGE Learning™

Detroit • New York • San Francisco • New Haven, Conn • Waterville, Maine • London

GALE
CENGAGE Learning

Elizabeth Des Chenes, *Managing Editor*

© 2012 Greenhaven Press, a part of Gale, Cengage Learning

Gale and Greenhaven Press are registered trademarks used herein under license.

For more information, contact:
Greenhaven Press
27500 Drake Rd.
Farmington Hills, MI 48331-3535
Or you can visit our Internet site at gale.cengage.com

ALL RIGHTS RESERVED.
No part of this work covered by the copyright herein may be reproduced, transmitted, stored, or used in any form or by any means graphic, electronic, or mechanical, including but not limited to photocopying, recording, scanning, digitizing, taping, Web distribution, information networks, or information storage and retrieval systems, except as permitted under Section 107 or 108 of the 1976 United States Copyright Act, without the prior written permission of the publisher.

For product information and technology assistance, contact us at

Gale Customer Support, 1-800-877-4253
For permission to use material from this text or product, submit all requests online at www.cengage.com/permissions

Further permissions questions can be emailed to permissionrequest@cengage.com

Articles in Greenhaven Press anthologies are often edited for length to meet page requirements. In addition, original titles of these works are changed to clearly present the main thesis and to explicitly indicate the author's opinion. Every effort is made to ensure that Greenhaven Press accurately reflects the original intent of the authors. Every effort has been made to trace the owners of copyrighted material.

Cover image copyright © iStockPhoto.com/andipantz.

LIBRARY OF CONGRESS CATALOGING-IN-PUBLICATION DATA

Welfare / Margaret Haerens, book editor.
    p. cm. -- (Opposing viewpoints)
    Includes bibliographical references and index.
    ISBN 978-0-7377-5430-8 (hbk.) -- ISBN 978-0-7377-5431-5 (pbk.)
    1. Public welfare--United States--Juvenile literature. I. Haerens, Margaret.
    HV91.W46632 2011
    362.5'5680973--dc23
                                                        2011021326

Printed in the United States of America
1 2 3 4 5 6 7 15 14 13 12 11

Contents

Chapter 1: Is Welfare Reform Working?

Chapter 2: How Has the Recession Affected Welfare?

Chapter 3: How Do Welfare Policies Affect Families?

**Chapter 4: What Are Some
Alternatives and Improvements
to the Welfare System?**

Why Consider Opposing Viewpoints?

> *"The only way in which a human being can make some approach to knowing the whole of a subject is by hearing what can be said about it by persons of every variety of opinion and studying all modes in which it can be looked at by every character of mind. No wise man ever acquired his wisdom in any mode but this."*
>
> *John Stuart Mill*

In our media-intensive culture it is not difficult to find differing opinions. Thousands of newspapers and magazines and dozens of radio and television talk shows resound with differing points of view. The difficulty lies in deciding which opinion to agree with and which "experts" seem the most credible. The more inundated we become with differing opinions and claims, the more essential it is to hone critical reading and thinking skills to evaluate these ideas. Opposing Viewpoints books address this problem directly by presenting stimulating debates that can be used to enhance and teach these skills. The varied opinions contained in each book examine many different aspects of a single issue. While examining these conveniently edited opposing views, readers can develop critical thinking skills such as the ability to compare and contrast authors' credibility, facts, argumentation styles, use of persuasive techniques, and other stylistic tools. In short, the Opposing Viewpoints Series is an ideal way to attain the higher-level thinking and reading skills so essential in a culture of diverse and contradictory opinions.

In addition to providing a tool for critical thinking, Opposing Viewpoints books challenge readers to question their own strongly held opinions and assumptions. Most people form their opinions on the basis of upbringing, peer pressure, and personal, cultural, or professional bias. By reading carefully balanced opposing views, readers must directly confront new ideas as well as the opinions of those with whom they disagree. This is not to simplistically argue that everyone who reads opposing views will—or should—change his or her opinion. Instead, the series enhances readers' understanding of their own views by encouraging confrontation with opposing ideas. Careful examination of others' views can lead to the readers' understanding of the logical inconsistencies in their own opinions, perspective on why they hold an opinion, and the consideration of the possibility that their opinion requires further evaluation.

Evaluating Other Opinions

To ensure that this type of examination occurs, Opposing Viewpoints books present all types of opinions. Prominent spokespeople on different sides of each issue as well as well-known professionals from many disciplines challenge the reader. An additional goal of the series is to provide a forum for other, less known, or even unpopular viewpoints. The opinion of an ordinary person who has had to make the decision to cut off life support from a terminally ill relative, for example, may be just as valuable and provide just as much insight as a medical ethicist's professional opinion. The editors have two additional purposes in including these less known views. One, the editors encourage readers to respect others' opinions—even when not enhanced by professional credibility. It is only by reading or listening to and objectively evaluating others' ideas that one can determine whether they are worthy of consideration. Two, the inclusion of such viewpoints encourages the important critical thinking skill of objectively evaluating an author's credentials and bias. This evaluation will illuminate an author's reasons for taking a particular stance on an issue and will aid in readers' evaluation of the author's ideas.

It is our hope that these books will give readers a deeper understanding of the issues debated and an appreciation of the complexity of even seemingly simple issues when good and honest people disagree. This awareness is particularly important in a democratic society such as ours in which people enter into public debate to determine the common good. Those with whom one disagrees should not be regarded as enemies but rather as people whose views deserve careful examination and may shed light on one's own.

Thomas Jefferson once said that "difference of opinion leads to inquiry, and inquiry to truth." Jefferson, a broadly educated man, argued that "if a nation expects to be ignorant and free ... it expects what never was and never will be." As individuals and as a nation, it is imperative that we consider the opinions of others and examine them with skill and discernment. The Opposing Viewpoints Series is intended to help readers achieve this goal.

David L. Bender and Bruno Leone,
Founders

Introduction

> "The moral question about poverty in America—How can a country like this allow it?—has an easy answer: we can't. The political question that follows—What can we do about it?—has always been more difficult."
>
> —Barack Obama,
> "Remarks of Senator Barack Obama:
> Changing the Odds for
> Urban America," July 18, 2007.

A major and far-reaching economic downturn hit the United States beginning in late 2007. One of the key reasons for the financial crisis was the collapse of the US housing market. For years, banks had made money off of subprime mortgages, which are loans to individuals who may not be able to afford them. When borrowers began to default on their loans in large numbers, the price of homes fell. Many owners were forced into foreclosure or opted to walk away from a bad investment. The large number of foreclosures further deteriorated the strength of US banking institutions. Years of shady financial dealings and practices had led the US banking system to financial instability. Even large financial institutions were affected: Lehman Brothers went bankrupt and Bear Stearns, Merrill Lynch, and Wachovia had to be sold to survive. More than one hundred mortgage lenders went bankrupt from 2007 to 2008. The crisis soon expanded from financial institutions and the housing market to other parts of the economy. Businesses closed, unemployment increased, state and local government revenues fell, the stock market plummeted, and consumer spending plunged. The US economy was in freefall by the end of 2008.

The federal government intervened forcefully to ensure that the recession would not deepen. One of the first major measures the George W. Bush administration took was the Emergency Economy Stabilization Act of 2008, also known as the bailout of the US banking system, on October 3, 2008. The most controversial component of the bailout was the Troubled Assets Relief Program (TARP), which allocated $700 billion to purchase distressed assets, particularly mortgage-backed securities. The money was also used to inject capital into the system and prevent further collapse of banking and financial institutions.

Another major government intervention in the economy was the American Recovery and Reinvestment Act (ARRA), also known as the Stimulus Act, which was enacted by the Barack Obama administration on February 17, 2009. A $900 billion economic stimulus package that aimed to create jobs, fuel consumer spending, and promote investment, the stimulus funds were directed to help the economy begin to recover from the economic downturn. The stimulus, however, proved to be a lightning rod for controversy.

One of the most contentious provisions of the stimulus package was the creation of a $5 billion emergency fund to help states pay for added welfare recipients, known as the Temporary Assistance for Needy Families (TANF) Emergency Fund. The fund was created as an emergency measure to help the rising numbers of individuals who were financially devastated by the economic crisis and needed government assistance. The TANF Emergency Fund reimbursed states for most of the costs of their growing welfare rolls and subsidized job programs. It also provided $87 billion to subsidize state Medicaid costs; increase spending on food stamps by 12 percent; distribute additional money for the federal school lunch program and the Women, Infants & Children (WIC) nutrition program, and provided tax cuts to low-income taxpayers.

Welfare

State and local lawmakers welcomed the additional funds, acknowledging the financial assistance was vital during a tough economic time. These lawmakers were also confronting budget crises of their own, and many state and local governments lacked the funds to help the increasing numbers of individuals and families that required government assistance—many for the first time. A temporary assistance program was the stopgap these states needed to help people who needed it.

There were numerous critics of the program, however. These opponents accused the Obama administration of designing the TANF Emergency Fund as a backdoor way to reverse the gains made by the welfare reform law of 1996. One of the main reforms of the welfare system had been to initiate a system in which state governments get block grants and administer their own welfare systems, thereby giving states a vested interest in reducing the number of people receiving benefits. Studies of welfare reform confirmed that states enacted stricter criteria on benefit eligibility and implemented time limits on how long families could receive welfare assistance. Reverting back to having the federal government in charge of disbursement, these critics argued, was an invitation to lax oversight, bloated welfare rolls, mismanagement, and a disincentive for states to get able-bodied individuals off of public assistance and into the workforce.

The controversy over the TANF Emergency Fund signaled its doom. In 2010 the program was set to expire, and the US Senate blocked every attempt to extend and renew it. Even though supporters argued that continued government assistance was vital in dire economic times, the TANF Emergency Fund was allowed to expire on September 30, 2010. There were numerous calls to reinstate the program, however, in spite of the strong political opposition to it.

The debate over the TANF Emergency Fund illuminates the larger discussion about the efficacy of welfare reform and the impact of the economic downturn on the welfare system in the United States. The authors of the viewpoints presented in *Opposing Viewpoints: Welfare* discuss the success and consequences of welfare reform in the following chapters: Is Welfare Reform Working? How Has the Recession Affected Welfare? How Do Welfare Policies Affect Families? and What Are Some Alternatives and Improvements to the Welfare System? The information in this book will inform the reader about recent and continuing controversies about welfare as well as offering insight into improvements and alternatives to the current system.

 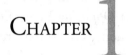

Is Welfare Reform Working?

Chapter Preface

By the mid-1990s many politicians, policymakers, and citizens were clamoring for an overhaul of the US welfare system. Conservative newspaper columnists, radio personalities, and television pundits expressed vitriol against welfare and other government assistance programs. They criticized abuses of the system, contending that welfare recipients committed fraud in order to pad benefits and eroded the integrity of the program. They questioned the need for a welfare system, claiming it only functioned to perpetuate dependence for people who needed to summon their own resources and energies to find work. Opponents observed that welfare was geared toward lazy and drug addicted people looking for an easy buck at the expense of hard-working Americans. Another criticism was that welfare paid women to have more babies and discouraged them from finding jobs. Many Americans found some degree of merit in these arguments, and during the 1980s and 1990s the issue of welfare reform was at the forefront of national political debate.

During the administration of president Bill Clinton the American government took decisive action on welfare reform. With the support of a Republican Congress, the Democratic president vowed to "end welfare as we know it." The result of that cooperation, the Personal Responsibility and Work Opportunity Act (PRWORA), was signed into law on August 22, 1996.

PRWORA signaled a fundamental change in the way government views and treats the welfare system. Under the old system, known as Aid to Families with Dependent Children (AFDC), the government offered federal cash assistance to low- or no-income families. The federal government provided the guidelines to the states, and the states administered the program. PRWORA eliminated AFDC, and replaced it with

Temporary Assistance for Needy Families (TANF), which gave states block grants and allowed them to both design and administer their own programs. TANF also put a five-year lifetime limit on welfare benefits and required welfare recipients to join the workforce after two years of receiving benefits. Some states enacted more stringent rules, reducing the amount of time welfare recipients could get benefits. It also aimed to encourage marriage and discourage out-of-wedlock births by greatly limiting the benefits of single parents under the age of eighteen.

Supporters of TANF and welfare reform applauded the shift toward work and away from entitlements. With recipients forced to leave the welfare system to seek employment after a designated time period, the number of people receiving welfare dropped significantly. Statistics show that between 1997 and 2000, almost half the number of recipients were dropped from the welfare system.

Some policymakers, however, view welfare reform as less than a success. They point out that welfare recipients who find work are often limited to low-paying jobs that place them in the category of the working poor. Many of these workers go without healthcare and childcare. These critics argue that stereotypes of welfare recipients are often based in racism and misogyny and tend to ignore the real struggle of people burdened by poverty, poor education, and a lack of opportunity. Instead, critics argue, these misconceptions further victimize and stigmatize people who need effective and comprehensive programs to find decent jobs and eventually obtain the American Dream for themselves and their families.

The debate over the efficacy of welfare reform is explored in the following chapter, which examines various aspects of welfare reform. Other issues discussed are the need for a new agenda to fight poverty and the value of welfare programs in general.

"[The] fact that Obama and his new HHS secretary have hardly been en- thusiastic in their support for welfare reform suggests that we may have to fight the battle for it all over again."

Welfare Reform Is Working

Steven Malanga

Steven Malanga is the senior editor of City Journal *and a senior fellow at the Manhattan Institute. In the following viewpoint, he underscores the major successes the 1996 welfare reform law has had in getting people off of welfare and back to work. Malanga praises the controversial reauthorization of the law in 2005, as- serting that it put even more people to work. Malanga discusses how some of the obstacles to getting people off of welfare have been overcome through tougher legislation, cooperation from employers and support organizations, and job training opportu- nities. He warns that such significant progress should not be tampered with by president Barack Obama and a Democratic Congress.*

As you read, consider the following questions:

1. Since 1996, how much have welfare caseloads plum- meted, according to Malanga?

Steven Malanga, "Welfare Reform, Phase Two," *City Journal*, Winter 2009. Reproduced by permission of Manhattan Institute for Policy Research.

2. According to Malanga, how many people are on the welfare rolls today?

3. What is "work-first," as explained in the viewpoint?

In social-services jargon, Debra Autry had "multiple barriers to work" when the state of Ohio told her that she had to start earning her welfare benefits. Autry had been out of work and on public assistance for more than two decades, and she lacked many of the skills necessary for a modern economy. She was a single mother, too, like most welfare recipients, with three kids at home. Autry was skeptical about working in the private sector, so the state placed her in a publicly subsidized program that had her cleaning government offices in exchange for her benefits. Disliking the work, Autry landed a cashier's job at a local Revco drugstore, arranging her hours around her children's school day. After the CVS chain bought out Revco, she enrolled in the company's program to learn how to become a pharmacy technician and eventually began working in that position, which typically pays between $25 and $30 per hour. Autry's hard work inspired her children. Her daughter just earned a degree as a physical therapist, while one son is in college and another is working full-time. "I was on welfare because there were no jobs that interested me," she recalls. "But once I had to go back to work, I realized there's a future if you want to better yourself. It was the best decision I ever made."

Autry's story is the kind that reformers dreamed about back in 1996, when President Bill Clinton signed the federal Personal Responsibility and Work Opportunity Reconciliation Act, often referred to as the welfare-reform act. That legislation, drawing on earlier innovations in Wisconsin and New York City, time-limited aid and required some recipients to work, seeking to end the culture of long-term dependency that no-strings-attached public assistance had helped foster. Autry's success story turned out to be one of many. Since

1996, welfare caseloads have plummeted by 70 percent—8.8 million people off the rolls, which today are down to 3.8 million.

In fact, during the first few years of welfare reform, the rolls fell so quickly that many state welfare agencies, which administer welfare for the federal government, stopped feeling pressure to move their remaining welfare clients back into the workforce. But since 2005, states have further reformed their welfare programs to comply with a controversial reauthorization of the 1996 legislation that required states to move even more people to work. This next, crucial phase of welfare reform could put an end to traditional cash welfare assistance in all but the most extreme cases.

That is, unless Democratic policymakers get in the way. Ominously, Democratic foes of welfare reform have gathered power both in Congress and in President Obama's cabinet.

Initial Successes

The 1996 welfare legislation gave states enormous flexibility in fulfilling its requirements, and many interpreted the law liberally. Some counted as "work" the hours that recipients spent in treatment for alcohol or drug addiction or in traveling to and from job-training sessions. Others let recipients satisfy work obligations by "helping a friend or relative with household tasks or errands," according to a 2005 Government Accountability Office study. Certain states allowed home exercise, "motivational reading," and antismoking classes to qualify recipients for aid, reasoning that such practices could at least lead to work.

Despite such laxity, 4 million welfare recipients left the rolls during the first two years after President Clinton signed the reform into law. Since many states previously had required virtually nothing of welfare clients, simply compelling them to meet with caseworkers to discuss work options was enough to propel many out the door to look for jobs. "Everyone underestimated the ability of single mothers to go back to work," says Grant Collins, former deputy director of the Office of Family Assistance in the Department of Health and Human Services (HHS).

The number of leavers was so big, in fact, that it all but eliminated many states' federal requirements to keep moving people off welfare. The legislation required states' work-participation rates—that is, the percentage of people on welfare who were working or searching for work—to be at least 50 percent. But states were allowed to diminish that fraction by whatever percentage their welfare rolls had shrunk since 1995. By 2002, welfare rolls nationwide had fallen so steeply that 33 states could meet their obligations with work-participation rates of less than 10 percent.

Tightening the Rules

That undesirable situation led to a three-year battle to reauthorize and reenergize welfare reform. The result was the 2005 Budget Reconciliation Act, which changed the year from which states could calculate case reductions from 1995 to 2005, thereby ending the generous credit that most states enjoyed from their huge initial drop in welfare cases. Between 40 and 50 percent of states' adult welfare recipients now had to go back to work, search for a job, or otherwise prepare to work. The federal government also tightened the definition of what counts in fulfilling the work requirement: no longer would spending time in psychological counseling or in traveling to job training do the trick. And the feds urged states to enroll more welfare recipients with physical or mental disabilities in job-training and job-placement programs. "Individuals who happen to have disabilities should be afforded the same opportunities to engage in work—to find work-related training, work experience, and employment—as those who do not have a disability," the Bush administration's Department of Health and Human Services wrote in its new regulations.

Advocates and some pols [politicians] charged that many of those remaining on welfare were too troubled for states to hit the demanding new work-participation targets. Urban League president Marc Morial complained that the bill would "subject families to harsher work requirements with inadequate funding" for social services to help them adjust. He scored the bill in particular for limiting how long someone could remain on welfare while pursuing a college degree. "We don't have many families left. Those remaining have multiple issues," objected the head of Welfare Advocates, a Maryland-based coalition of social-services agencies and churches. A 2002 Urban Institute study that found that 44 percent of welfare recipients faced two or more "barriers to work" became a frequent citation.

HHS had basically discounted such complaints in writing its new welfare regulations, in part because the critics were defining "barrier to work" too loosely. The Urban Institute study, for instance, considered the lack of a high school diploma, being out of the workforce for three or more years, and lack of English proficiency as obstacles to work, while other groups argued that being a single parent was a major barrier. A common demand was that welfare programs first provide day-care services for single parents or treatment for addicts before requiring any work. "I was at a White House conference in the mid-1990s in which someone observed that we couldn't require single mothers on welfare to go back to work until we had day care for all of them," recalls Peter Cove, cofounder of America Works, an employment service for welfare recipients. "I stood up and said that if we tried to solve every problem before asking people to work, we'd never get any recipient back in the workforce."

The Work-First Philosophy

The 2005 bill wholly embraced this "work-first" philosophy. Work-first originally emerged as a welfare-reform model in the 1980s, adopted by Wisconsin governor Tommy Thompson; in the mid-nineties, Mayor Rudy Giuliani enthusiastically signed on in New York City. At its core, work-first maintains that the biggest obstacle that many welfare clients face to employment is their own lack of understanding of the fundamentals of any workplace—showing up for work regularly and on time, for instance. The best way to help such people isn't to put them in elaborate job-training programs, this approach holds, but simply to get them working—even in entry-level positions—under the careful supervision of a caseworker, who makes sure that they get up in the morning and out the door. Caseworkers will even help out with recipients' child-care emergencies or get alcoholic clients to continue in treatment—but all with the aim of keeping them on the job. "Many of the best therapeutic programs for people with problems like alcoholism don't think it's a good idea for people to stop working and go home and sit on a couch all day after counseling," says Tom Steinhauser, head of Virginia's welfare division. "Why should welfare programs treat people any different?"

A work-first approach has helped sustain deep reductions in New York City's welfare population, long after rolls stopped dropping in some states. By the time Rudy Giuliani left office in 2001, the city's welfare numbers had fallen from 1.1 million to 475,000, and they're down another 25 percent, to 339,000, under Mayor Michael Bloomberg, who has continued the reforms. Many of those who wind up on welfare today remain "work-ready," argues Robert Doar, commissioner of Gotham's Human Resources Administration (HRA), which is why the city has been able to place some 70,000 to 80,000 of them a year in jobs.

The "work-ready" population is evident at the crowded Manhattan offices of America Works, where I went to observe cofounder Lee Bowes address a new group enrolled in the organization's counseling and employment program. Every seat is taken, and even the windowsills are occupied. When one attendee asks why the classroom is so crowded, Bowes bluntly responds: It's because lots of people are looking for jobs. Asked by Bowes how she wound up on welfare, a single mother explains that her apartment building burned and that she and her children found themselves temporarily homeless. She then lost her job and went on public assistance; she says that she's ready, though, to get back to work. Is this the first agency that she has visited since going on welfare, Bowes wonders? The woman's answer elicits nods from the group: "I went somewhere where they treated me like I was in kindergarten. They asked me if I was ready to go back to work. I said yes—can you help me find a job? Then I heard that this place does that. So I'm here now."

The Road to Financial Independence

Most of these welfare recipients will wind up in entry-level jobs. The average starting wage for someone coming off welfare in New York is just slightly above $9 an hour, according to the HRA. But with other assistance, like the federal and state earned income-tax credits, food stamps, and Medicaid, a recipient's actual annual income can rise well above $20,000— not enough for an extravagant lifestyle in New York, of course, but enough to allow her to get back on her feet and start down the road to independence. This aid menu is typical across the country, even if assistance levels vary. With the decline in welfare rolls, states now spend more on noncash assistance programs, like food stamps, than on welfare itself.

Many employers have tapped this labor pool because it has been hard for them to fill entry-level positions. New York City-sponsored job fairs for welfare recipients attract dozens of companies. America Works says that it has a reliable list of employers ready to hire welfare recipients for entry-level jobs. Even in an economic downturn, like the current one or the national recession that began in mid-2001, employers keep

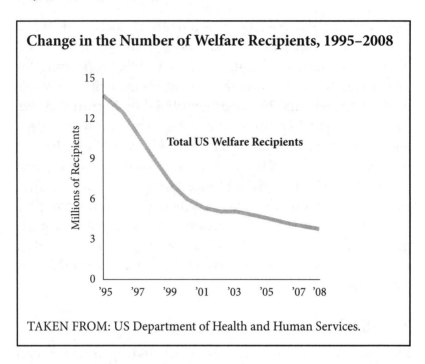

Change in the Number of Welfare Recipients, 1995–2008

Total US Welfare Recipients

Millions of Recipients

TAKEN FROM: US Department of Health and Human Services.

seeking entry-level workers because of the high turnover rate for these jobs. Welfare rolls didn't rise in New York City during the last recession, it's worth noting.

One of those eager entry-level employers is CVS, which has hired about 63,000 people off welfare nationwide over the last decade or so. Some 60 percent still work for the chain, an extraordinary statistic for an industry with high turnover. The typical former welfare recipient at CVS has had at least two promotions. Some, like Autry, have gone through training in CVS's pharmacy technician program; others have returned to school with the chain's help and earned pharmacist's degrees. One key to their success with former welfare recipients, CVS has learned, is to work closely with state agencies and their contractors, who'll lend a hand with the new hires for several months or longer to ease their transition to employment. "We learned early on that you just don't throw someone into a full-time job right away without some support," says Steve

Wing, director of workforce initiatives at CVS. "We rely on the agencies to help these people adjust."

Many state agencies and advocacy groups have derided entry-level jobs in retailing or in service industries—the places where welfare recipients will most likely find work—as pointless, "dead-end" employment. It was this foolish and hoary objection, dating back to the welfare debates of the seventies, that for years thwarted efforts to get welfare recipients working. "We heard the line about dead-end jobs so often from people running welfare agencies that we drew up a poster showing the career opportunities for people at CVS who start by working as cashiers in stores," says Wing. "The stores are where a lot of our managerial employees start, but there's just a perception among those who run welfare programs that these entry-level jobs are not good enough."

Getting People to Work

Under the revised welfare rules, however, states can no longer ignore such employers and their jobs, and more states are reshaping their programs along work-first lines. Over the last two years, for instance, 17 states have created more stringent contracts for local private agencies working with welfare recipients, requiring them to meet job-placement targets or risk penalties. Arizona has told its contractors that if the federal government penalizes the state for failing to meet work goals, the contractors must share in the punishment. Private groups must even prove when bidding for Arizona contracts that they have sufficient financial reserves to pay any fines. But the state will also give bonuses to agencies that perform job placement well.

Several states have imposed stricter standards even on their own public agencies. In California, new legislation lets the state pass on to county welfare offices any financial penalties that it might incur for failing to meet the new federal regulations. County administrators also must file plans explaining how they intend to meet their new requirements, and county work-participation rates now get shared throughout the system, so everyone can see how each county is performing. Pennsylvania, which had a dismal 7 percent work-participation rate for its approximately 40,000 adult welfare recipients in 2005, not only has started grading each county program but publishes the entire list online.

States are also requiring welfare applicants to begin job searches or undergo employment counseling much more quickly than in the past. Eleven states have altered application procedures to include some kind of employment assessment for people when they first request welfare. New applicants in Delaware, for instance, must spend two weeks working with an employment and training counselor before receiving benefits. Missouri no longer considers a welfare application complete unless the applicant has met with an employment counselor and worked out a job-search plan.

Impose Penalties for Non-Compliance

In many states, welfare recipients once could keep getting benefits even when they refused to comply with work or vocational requirements, an enormous impediment to reform. Since the 2005 legislation, however, ten states that previously only partially reduced a welfare recipient's check for failing to participate in such programs have now moved to "full sanctions," that is, cutting off benefits completely. Other states, while not going as far, have implemented harsher penalties or are at least considering doing so.

Welfare programs are also launching more joint private-public training ventures, aimed at funneling recipients directly into jobs. Welfare and employment agencies in Atlanta, Baltimore, Cleveland, Detroit, and Washington, D.C. have tapped CVS, because of its previous experience hiring former welfare clients, to establish training centers—essentially, replicas of its stores—where recipients can prepare for full-time jobs at the chain. Hawaii has formed a similar partnership with local banks, resulting in more than 300 welfare recipients' getting placed in permanent jobs. New York City has joined with cable TV and phone companies to train welfare recipients as customer-service representatives.

Assessing the Problem Cases

Agencies are also taking a harder look at programs that try to get those who claim to have physical or mental barriers to work on the path toward employment. Sometimes this means encouraging them to begin part-time work or to undergo counseling to see what kind of training and work they might qualify for. "States are doing things that sound really simple, like having their own doctors assess those who claim they can't work," says Jason Turner, who designed Wisconsin's welfare-to-work programs and is now a Milwaukee-based consultant. "But you would be surprised how many states were merely accepting notes from a welfare recipient's doctor, excusing them from work."

One model is WeCare, which handles New York City's toughest cases. Welfare recipients who say they can't work are enrolled in this program, in which a city-employed doctor and a caseworker evaluate them. If the doctor decides that a person can work but has a condition—a bad back or asthma, say—that restricts the types of jobs he can do, the caseworker draws up a job-search plan based on those limitations. Welfare recipients not well enough to work immediately but not permanently disabled are put on a treatment regimen to get them healthier and employable. "If they are exempt from work, they must still participate in treatments and in vocational rehabilitation programs," says Michael Bosket, who heads WeCare. "Everyone does something."

Typically, about 6 percent of the recipients referred to We-Care are deemed employable and sent directly back to a caseworker to find a job; another 43 percent are found employable with limitations. "Many people who used to be considered having barriers to work really have barriers to certain kinds of jobs, but they shouldn't be exempt from work," says Cove. Of the nearly 24,000 people in the WeCare program last fall, about 3,000 worked or enrolled in approved work-participation programs, about 7,000 were undergoing treatment or vocational therapy, and some 8,500 had been judged permanently disabled by the city's doctors and directed to apply for federal disability benefits, which are separate from the welfare system. (The rest of the WeCare group was still undergoing evaluation.)

An Uncertain Future

The new law gave states two years to comply, starting from mid-2006, when the feds issued the specific regulations outlining states' obligations. Many states, including Pennsylvania, Maryland, and Virginia, say that they've raised their work-participation rates substantially since then and are close to complying, though the feds have yet to issue a report on the states' progress.

Yet no one knows how Barack Obama's White House—which brings with it a whole new set of administrators at the Department of Health and Human Services under the new secretary, former Senate majority leader Tom Daschle [Daschle withdrew his nomination in 2009]—will carry out the law. As a senator, Daschle opposed the original 1996 welfare reform and then stalled its reauthorization from 2002 through his 2004 electoral defeat. Obama, meanwhile, turned down several opportunities during the presidential campaign to say whether he would have signed the welfare-reform act if he had been president in 1996; he preferred not to look back, he said, but forward. During the campaign, he did run ads crediting the 1997 Illinois law that he helped write—which brought the state's welfare system in line with federal changes—with Illinois' decline in welfare caseloads.

Congress's most powerful Democrats have also opposed welfare reform. Speaker of the House Nancy Pelosi voted against both the 1996 legislation (calling it "punitive and unrealistic") and the 2005 bill. Harry Reid, the current Senate majority leader, has used language strikingly similar to that of social-services advocates to criticize welfare reform. On its tenth anniversary, he declared that "many welfare recipients face significant barriers to employment" and that states need "flexibility" in aiding them.

At the very least, such statements suggest that a Reid-and-Pelosi-controlled Congress could unwind some key elements of the 2005 law, such as the restrictions on counting certain kinds of job training or substance-abuse counseling as work, when welfare reform again comes up for reauthorization in 2011. Such moves would almost certainly inflate work-participation rates artificially and blunt some of the effectiveness of the 2005 reforms. Whether Congress would attempt to go further, digging into the original 1996 legislation and curtailing some of its mandates, is hard to predict at this stage. But the fact that Obama and his new HHS secretary have hardly been enthusiastic in their support for welfare reform suggests that we may have to fight the battle for it all over again.

| "While welfare reform was long ago declared a success in some quarters, it was deeply flawed from the beginning."

Welfare Reform Is Not Working

Barbara Ehrenreich and Peter Edelman

Peter Edelman is a professor at Georgetown Law Center and served as an assistant secretary of Health and Human Services in the Bill Clinton administration. Barbara Ehrenreich is an author and newspaper columnist. In the following viewpoint, they contend that America's 1996 experiment with welfare reform was a failure. Edelman and Ehrenreich argue that reform "was based on reckless assumptions about the economy, as well as a callous disregard for the realities of sustaining a family." They illustrate their contention that the economic recession has devastated many families that could have been helped with welfare assistance, and maintain that current policies on welfare benefits are unjust and often inhumane.

As you read, consider the following questions:

1. How many people do the authors indicate were served by food stamps in 2009?

Barbara Ehrenreich and Peter Edelman, "Why Welfare Reform Has Failed," *Washington Post*, December 6, 2009. Reproduced by permission of the author.

2. According to the US government, how many Americans were experiencing "food insecurity" in 2009?

3. How much did the number of people living in extreme poverty increase from 2000 to 2008, according to the statistics cited by the authors?

We all like to imagine that there'll be something to stop our fall if we hit hard times. Mulugeta Yimer, for example, is a 56-year-old Alexandria cabdriver who escaped poverty and persecution in Ethiopia 20 years ago only to be clobbered by the recession. Business is way down, and he's facing possible foreclosure on his home. He says he is averse to government handouts, but when he contemplates what might be in store for his wife, who works part-time at a convenience store, and their two young children, he muses wistfully, "There's always welfare, isn't there?"

Actually, no. When President Bill Clinton signed welfare reform into law, he didn't just end welfare as we knew it. For all practical purposes, it turned out, he brought an end to cash help of any kind for families with children in much of the country. While welfare reform was long ago declared a success in some quarters, it was deeply flawed from the beginning. The recession has shown how seriously unprepared it left us for hard times.

Conservatives had been attacking the old welfare system for decades, claiming that it fostered dependency. Many liberals found it unsatisfactory as well. Welfare checks weren't big enough to lift families out of poverty, and the system did little to help recipients get or keep jobs. When Republicans gained control of Congress and welfare rolls swelled in the early 1990s, these attacks gained momentum, and in 1996, Clinton ended the legal right to cash assistance and imposed a five-year limit on federally financed help to any given family.

Welfare reform also provided the states with nearly complete discretion over how to administer benefits. Most states responded with gusto, reducing welfare rolls nationally by two-thirds in just a few years.

The Impact of the Recession

So when the Great Recession came along, the government safety net for families with children was in tatters. The United States was no more prepared for massive unemployment than New Orleans had been prepared for its levees to fail. Some important government programs, including unemployment insurance and food stamps, have started to rise to the challenge and have even begun to lose their stigma among former members of the middle class. Unemployment insurance now covers 57 percent of those who have lost their jobs, as opposed to less than 40 percent before the recession—although their benefits amount to less half their former wages. Reliance on food stamps has expanded even more dramatically. While the average benefit still isn't enough to meet people's basic nutritional needs, the program now serves 36 million people, double the number when Clinton left office and up by a quarter in the past year.

By contrast, the caseload for TANF (Temporary Assistance for Needy Families, the name we now give welfare) is about 5 million people. This number is up by about 1 million since the beginning of the recession, but it's still just a little over a third of what it was 15 years ago, before welfare reform.

Food Stamps vs. Welfare

Why the huge difference between unemployment insurance and food stamp usage and welfare caseloads? People have a legal right to food stamps if they meet the statutory requirements, but since 1996 there has been no legal right to cash assistance. And so welfare, generally speaking, has not cushioned the impact of the recession.

We can see the results: According to the National Law Center on Homelessness & Poverty, the number of homeless Americans is up by 61 percent since the recession began in December 2007. That figure will only continue to rise. The number of people living in poverty increased by 2.5 million during the first year of the recession, and it has surely risen further in 2009. The government reported recently that nearly 50 million Americans are experiencing what it delicately calls "food insecurity."

We are among the co-authors of a forthcoming report from the Institute for Policy Studies titled *Battered by the Storm*, which documents the government's inadequate response to the human suffering caused by the recession and describes the excruciating choices people now face between feeding their families and paying the rent.

Worst Fears Have Been Realized

Both of us were critical of the new approach to welfare when it was enacted in 1996. One of us resigned from the government in protest of the law; the other helped organize opposition to it from within the women's movement. We argued that the low-wage jobs available to former welfare recipients would not pay the bills. We warned that the legislation didn't provide adequate child care for single mothers thrown off welfare. And we cautioned that many welfare recipients faced serious barriers to success in the job market.

But some advocates of welfare reform seemed to consider poverty a voluntary condition, one curable with a quick kick in the pants and the opportunity to work for minimum wage. There were not enough jobs even then, but, blinded by the economic boom of the 1990s, the authors of TANF seemed to think that the business cycle had been abolished and that prosperity would take us only onward and upward.

The Welfare System Is Not Working

From the newspaper headlines to the consensus of small-town conversations, it is clear that most Americans feel that the system is not working, and many of those who are on assistance programs are taking advantage of major flaws when it comes to services to low-income families. Is the problem rooted in too many services provided with not enough oversight? Have low-income families become too adept at scamming the system? Should these programs be dismantled and their funding allocated elsewhere?

Joel Troxell, "Does Welfare Work?
Why the System Has Failed America's Poor,"
Associated Content, *October 28, 2007.*

More Working Poor

In the rapidly expanding service economy of the 1990s, many former welfare recipients did find jobs, but most did not escape poverty, and a significant number were pushed off the rolls without finding work. Research showed that one in five former recipients ultimately became disconnected from any means of support: They no longer had welfare, but they didn't have jobs. They hadn't married or moved in with a partner or family, and they weren't getting disability benefits. And so, after a decline in the late 1990s, the number of people living in extreme poverty (with an income less than half the poverty line, or below about $9,100 for a family of three) shot up by more than a third, from 12.6 million in 2000 to 17.1 million in 2008.

In some states TANF virtually disappeared—perhaps not surprisingly, given the states' new discretion and pressure from

Washington to slash the rolls. Nationally, the fraction of poor children getting help plummeted from almost two-thirds to less than a third. A number of states reduced their welfare rolls by 90 percent.

Is Welfare Reform Working?

Perversely, many observers welcomed these huge declines as proof that welfare reform was working. They didn't bother to follow these families as they moved into ever more crowded living situations, pieced together patchworks of part-time jobs or left their children alone while they went to work.

With the recession that began at the end of 2001, thousands of women who'd been removed from the rolls found themselves without jobs or welfare. Beverly Ransom, for example—a Miami welfare reform "success story"—had found well-paying work in the catering business, until the recession took her job away and left her without employment prospects and unable to pay rent for herself and her two children on the meager assistance available to her. She eventually found help from a community organization fighting for welfare rights.

If 2001 and the months thereafter revealed holes in the safety net, the current crisis shows even more vividly that TANF is essentially irrelevant in large parts of the country. If the real purpose of welfare reform was simply to reduce the rolls, it's been a smashing success. Some states have been more responsive to economic conditions, but they are the exception. Even now, in the face of high unemployment, caseloads in many states are tiny. At the end of last year, Wyoming had 281 families on its rolls—about 550 people. Idaho had 1,600 families, Oklahoma had 8,639, and Arkansas had 8,664. The share of poor families receiving TANF was 4 percent in Wyoming, 5 percent in Idaho, 9 percent in Illinois, 9 percent in Louisiana and 9 percent in Texas. Caseloads fell in 20 states during 2008.

Benefits are tiny, too, with 30 states paying a maximum benefit that's less than 30 percent of the federal poverty line.

Mississippi skimps by offering its TANF recipients $170 a month for a family of three, about 9 percent of the poverty line and barely enough to cover the utility bills.

No Money for Aid

Nationwide, there has been no increase in federal welfare funding since the 1996 law was enacted, so thanks to inflation, the value of that funding has eroded by about a third. There is an emergency fund for TANF in the stimulus package Congress passed in February, but little of it has been spent, primarily because it requires a match that fiscally strapped states are unable to put on the table.

Most states in effect adopted a welfare policy of ignoring the recession. Fourteen of 24 states that responded to an Urban Institute survey this fall said they had not changed any of their TANF policies or practices in response to higher unemployment.

Keeping Welfare Rolls Down

There are two techniques that allowed states to radically reduce welfare rolls over the past decade, and they are being used to keep the rolls down now, even as need escalates. The first is to shut the front door almost completely through a process called "diversion"—essentially telling someone: "You look able-bodied. Go out and look for a job." The Urban Institute's analysis showed that 42 states have rules that discourage enrollment, such as requiring an extensive job search, even when there are obviously no jobs to be found. For a person without a car or access to public transportation, a requirement to apply for dozens of jobs before an application for welfare will even be considered, as some states and counties mandate, can be a deal-breaker.

In some states, according to Kaaryn Gustafson of the University of Connecticut law school, "applying for welfare is a lot like being booked for a crime." There may be a mug shot, fingerprinting and lengthy interrogations as to the true paternity of one's children. Word gets around, and, even in the face of destitution, many people will not undergo such indignities.

The other technique for keeping the rolls down is to staff the back door with the equivalent of a nightclub bouncer. The practice is called "sanctioning"—kicking people off the rolls because they were late to a work assignment (no excuses accepted, whether for sick children, late buses or car trouble) or didn't show up for an appointment at the welfare office (no dispensation for failure to receive notice of an appointment or inability to understand English). In some states multiple infractions of this sort can result in lifetime disqualification.

Reform Is a Failure

It's time to acknowledge that America's 1996 experiment with welfare reform was based on reckless assumptions about the economy, as well as a callous disregard for the realities of sustaining a family. We need a massive emergency relief package not only to fund new jobs but to repair the grievous holes in our national safety net. Fifty million people need help now— not in three months or six months, but today.

VIEWPOINT 3

| "Yes, welfare reform reduced welfare de-
pendency, but not as much as suggested
by the political rhetoric."

Welfare Reform Has Had Mixed Results

Douglas J. Besharov

Douglas J. Besharov is the Joseph J. and Violet Jacobs Scholar in Social Welfare Studies at the American Enterprise Institute. In the following viewpoint, he argues that the results of welfare reform are mixed. Besharov suggests that although the number of caseloads dropped in every state, they did so because of the strong economy more than because of welfare reform. He also notes that welfare reform did not reduce welfare dependency as much as reform supporters claim it did. Besharov adds that current welfare laws could benefit families if the laws were not circumvented by states trying to reduce their expenditures, and maintains that the true level of dependency is unclear because of such avoidance tactics.

As you read, consider the following questions:

1. How much does Besharov state that welfare caseloads have fallen since welfare reform efforts began in 1996?

Douglas J. Besharov, "Two Cheers for Welfare Reform," *AEI*, August 22, 2006. Reproduced by permission of the author.

2. By what percentage did welfare caseloads rise between 1989 and 1994, according to the author?

3. What percentage of mothers who left welfare have steady, full-time jobs, according to Besharov?

It has been nearly ten years since President Bill Clinton signed the landmark 1996 welfare reform law. The anniversary has been the occasion for various news stories and opinion pieces, most of them praising the law's success in reducing welfare dependency.

And it is true: welfare caseloads have fallen an astounding 60 percent since reform efforts began. But even as a strong supporter of welfare reform, I find it difficult to muster unqualified enthusiasm for the law and how it has been implemented.

In the years immediately before the law's passage, welfare dependency seemed out of control. Between 1989 and 1994, for example, caseloads rose a worrisome 34 percent. Analysts argued over how much to blame the weak economy, worsening social problems (primarily nonmarital births and drug addiction), and lax agency administration. But few claimed that another 1.3 million people on welfare was a good thing.

Mixed Results

Responding to the growing concern about welfare dependency, Clinton campaigned for president on a promise to "end welfare as we know it." But he had in mind something far different from what the Republicans handed him in 1996. Nevertheless, to the chagrin of his liberal allies, he signed the legislation that ended the welfare entitlement and gave states wide discretion in running the program, as long as they put 50 percent of recipients in work-related activities and imposed a five-year limit on financial aid.

Many feared a social calamity. Senator Daniel Patrick Moynihan (D-N.Y.), widely respected for his decades-long study of welfare, warned that the law would "push 1.1 million children into poverty" and that we would "have children sleeping on grates." But in the years since, although researchers have strived mightily, they have found only small pockets of additional hardship. Not a happy finding, but far from the "Grate Society," as people called Moynihan's prediction. Even better, the earnings of most single mothers actually rose.

These twin realities—decreased caseloads and little sign of serious additional hardship—are why both Republicans and Democrats think welfare reform has been a success.

Facing Reality

But the results are more mixed. Caseloads fell sharply in all states, yet they did so seemingly regardless of what actions the state took. They fell in states with strong work-first requirements and those without them, in states with mandatory work programs and those without them, in states with job training programs and those without them, and in states with generous child care subsidies and those without them. They just fell.

In fact, the consensus among academic researchers is that it took more than welfare reform to end welfare as we knew it. If one looks at all the studies, the most reasonable conclusion is that, although welfare reform was an important factor in caseload reduction (accounting for 25 to 35 percent of the decline), the strong economy was probably more important (35 to 45 percent). Expanded aid to low-income, working families (primarily through the Earned Income Tax Credit) was almost as important (20 to 30 percent).

Moreover, the best estimates are that only about 40 to 50 percent of mothers who left welfare have steady, full-time jobs. Another 15 percent or so work part-time. According to surveys in various states, these mothers are earning about $8 an hour. That's about $16,000 a year for full-time employment. It is their story that the supporters of welfare reform celebrate, but $16,000 is not a lot of money, especially for a mother with two children (about the average number of children for those leaving welfare).

Clandestine Welfare

What about the other 50 percent of families who left without a regular job? Neither the Left nor the Right likes to dwell on them, because they tend to undercut each side's rhetoric: Some families did not "need" welfare, perhaps because they were living with parents or a boyfriend, and they simply left when work requirements were imposed. And some families left welfare only because of intense pressure from caseworkers. ("Hassle" is often a more accurate description.) About a quarter of those who leave welfare return, with many cycling in and out as they face temporary ups and downs.

When they are off welfare, many of these families survive only because they still receive government assistance through, for example, food stamps (an average of more than $2,500 per year); the Women, Infants and Children program (WIC) (about $1,800 for infants and new mothers per year); Supplemental Security Income (an average of over $6,500 per year); or housing aid (an average of $6,000 per year). Their children also qualify for Medicaid. In reality, these families are still on welfare because they are still receiving benefits and not working—call it "welfare lite."

Poverty and Dependence Still Exist

So, yes, welfare reform reduced welfare dependency, but not as much as suggested by the political rhetoric—and a great deal of dependency is now diffused and hidden within larger social welfare programs. As a result, public and political concern about dependency has largely disappeared (a point often celebrated by welfare advocates). This has obscured the precarious financial situation of these unfortunate families and blunted the political impetus to address the underlying causes of poverty, from inadequate schools and structural shifts in the economy to family breakdown and other forms of social dysfunction.

The newly reauthorized welfare law could help—if states used its tougher work and participation requirements to address the deeper needs of welfare families. With the help of the federal government, the states could develop programs that discourage nonmarital births (especially among teens), encourage stronger families, and build human capital through work experience and job training programs. But many states are already planning to avoid these new strictures by various administrative gimmicks, like placing the most troubled and disorganized families in state-financed programs where federal rules do not apply. This would only further obscure the high levels of continuing dependency.

For now, welfare reform deserves only two cheers. Not bad for a historic change in policy, but not good enough for us to be even close to satisfied.

> *"Frankly, I am fine with a nation that does not feed people who are not willing to work."*

Welfare Reform Has Not Gone Far Enough

Craig R. Smith

Craig R. Smith is an author and conservative commentator. In the following viewpoint, he asserts that despite attempts to reform welfare, the system is in trouble again. Smith argues that it is time to reevaluate a system that allows unproductive citizens to receive government assistance. He believes it is time to get tough with all government assistance programs. His suggestions for stricter policies include instituting surveillance of recipients to crack down on cases of fraud; taking payment for emergency medical treatment for the uninsured out of future earnings or welfare benefits; and sending medical bills for illegal immigrants to their native countries for payment.

As you read, consider the following questions:

1. What percentage of American households does Smith maintain depend on some form of income from the government?

Craig R. Smith, "Let the Pains Begin," WorldNetDaily.com, November 15, 2010. Reproduced by permission of WND.com Inc.

2. How many working Americans pay into Social Security for every one recipient as of 2003, according to Smith?

3. How many additional baby boomers does Smith indicate were about to get SSI benefits at the beginning of 2010?

The time has come in America to let the pains begin.

Over the last 87 years our politicians have been slowly building a welfare state in America with an abundance of unproductive takers and a steadily increasing deficiency of productive participants.

With 42 million Americans now receiving food stamps and 50 percent of all households depending on some form of income from the government, just how long do we think we can keep the system afloat? How many more nonproductive citizens, who have grown very accustomed to their bills being paid by the government, can we add before our system collapses under its own weight?

FDR [US president Franklin Delano Roosevelt] introduced the first of many government dependence programs falsely called "Social Security." By 1950, there were 16 working Americans paying into the system for every one beneficiary. By 2003, there were 3.3 contributors for every one recipient. It is projected by 2033 that ratio will be 2:1. That is a system with a low chance of survival.

Social Security Is Doomed to Fail

This admonition was offered by [US Federal Reserve chairman] Alan Greenspan in February 2004 in a AP [Associated Press] story: "As 77 million of the baby boom generation become eligible for Social Security starting in 2008, this dramatic demographic change is certain to place enormous demands . . . demands we will almost surely be unable to meet unless action is taken . . . as soon as possible, the country will go from having just over three workers supporting each retiree to 2.25 workers for every retiree by 2025."

He was right!

I know what you are going to say. There is a trust fund. Once we start taking in less than we pay out, we tap the trust. Wrong sparky! Your wonderful politicians spent the money. There is no "lock box." The FICA payments paid were spent just like every other tax dollar.

Social Security was a tax spent wastefully and foolishly by a bunch of nit wits thinking they could make a program work. But it was doomed from the start.

But that is just one of the many programs destined to fail.

As the number of illegal aliens receiving free medical care and social services increases, how long will it be until other states face what the bankrupted state of California is facing? So much for the unbridled success of "sanctuary cities."

We have come to a point in America when we just need to say no!

Just Say No

Will it be painful? Very! No doubt. But it is surely coming and steps must be taken immediately if we are to remain a nation with freedom and liberty. The ability to succeed or fail is the backbone of freedom and anything short of that is slavery in a glossy wrapper.

I know we don't want people dying in the streets for lack of medical care, and I doubt America's image in the world would improve if photos of starving people living on the street were broadcast like the pictures from Abu Ghraib. However, we must come to grips with reality. We cannot afford to pay for all this care for everyone who allegedly needs it.

It is now clear that, without substantial entitlement reform, it is impossible to stop future deterioration of the economic wellbeing of the country. We just can't continue to pro-

"Welfare Pidgeons," cartoon by Andy Singer, PoliticalCartoons.com, May 5, 2010. Copyright © 2010 Andy Singer, PoliticalCartoons.com. All rights reserved.

vide what many have grown accustom to receiving. The math no longer works. The day is rapidly approaching were we must face the music.

For far too long we have avoided these burdens to our budget. Social Security, Medicaid, Medicare and welfare have been "reformed" several times in the past only to be in crisis years later. That should make us question the viability of these programs going forward. I know the intentions were mostly pure, but we can't afford them. The pathway to hell is paved with good intentions.

Time to Get Tough

Frankly, I am fine with a nation that does not feed people who are not willing to work. I have no problem putting someone out on the street when they believe they are entitled to be taken care of because of where they were born. Not everyone who claims he or she needs help should get it, only those who truly do. How many times have you watched a person on disability busted by a camera crew as they are boarding a ski lift or playing softball when they claim they can't walk? There are many people willing to lie to get a check.

I am fine with people who walk into a ER [Emergency Room] expecting to receive free treatment being told no. Or at least being handed a bill when they leave. They can pay the bill slowly out of their future earnings. Or at least a percentage of the winning lottery ticket they bought with their welfare check.

Maybe sending a bill to the country of origin's government for the illegals who receive care would be appropriate. Why should you and I have to pay? I didn't ask them to break into our country.

With 42 million citizens on food stamps and 50 percent of households requiring some form of government assistance, we have an unsustainable economic model for our country. Unless that country is willing to trade its freedom and liberty for the promise of a hot meal, a roof and medical care.

Soon we will have an additional 77 million baby boomers getting SSI benefits and millions more on unemployment. Add to that the millions on welfare and disability. At what point do we say *no mas*?!

Elections Have Consequences

On Nov. 2 [2010] the people spoke. They want less government, less spending and balanced budgets. They voted for people who would make tough decisions to get America back on track.

[Speaker of the House of Representatives] Nancy Pelosi's response to the tough decisions will be as it was last week, "Well, that is just unacceptable." Frankly Ms. Pelosi, we couldn't care less what you think. You are now irrelevant. It is you and your liberal pals who got us into this mess.

So get to work [Washington,] D.C. You have been assigned a task by the American people. A task that would have been a lot less painful if it had been handled decades ago. But it was ignored. Now the time has come for the pains to begin.

> "The challenge is to develop a set of poli-
> cies that . . . provide both opportunity
> to help poor people get into the main-
> stream of the economy and security
> against the harsh disruptions of that
> economy and of life in general."

A New Agenda Is Needed to Fight Poverty

Mark Schmitt and Shelley Waters Boots

Mark Schmitt is the executive editor of The American Prospect, *and Shelley Waters Boots is a philanthropic consultant. In the following viewpoint, they contend that in light of the recession, it is time to bring attention to the plight of the poor in this country. The authors maintain that because economic circumstances have changed dramatically in the last few decades, policies need to be adjusted accordingly. Schmitt and Boots outline some recent anti-poverty initiatives and argue that it is the right time to make poverty reduction a top priority.*

As you read, consider the following questions:

1. What event do Schmitt and Boots say drew into sharp relief the fragility of life for poor families?

Mark Schmitt and Shelley Waters Boots, "A New Agenda for Tough Times," *The American Prospect*, September 14, 2009. Reproduced by permission.

2. What has happened to the teen pregnancy rate since 2005, according to the authors?

3. How many children do the authors state lived below half the poverty line in 2005?

It has been 13 years since a Democratic president's signature on the Personal Responsibility and Work Opportunity Reconciliation Act of 1996 eliminated a flawed program that also provided the only protection against destitution. Yet that act also brought an end to the welfare wars, a long and debilitating period in which poor people were the focus of political conflict and racially loaded demagoguery, exemplified by former Sen. Phil Gramm's image of a society divided between those "pulling the wagon" and those "riding in the wagon." Even liberals stepped with trepidation, insisting that they, too, would end welfare as we knew it.

In the years since, absent a high-profile conflict over policy, poverty has once again become invisible. As Michael Harrington wrote in 1962, "That the poor are invisible is one of the most important things about them." But there is a sense that the shadows are lifting. Hurricane Katrina's devastating effects on New Orleans and the Gulf Coast briefly drew into sharp relief the fragility of life for poor families, as well as the inescapable racial dimension of poverty. The Center for American Progress put forward a major initiative in 2007, outlining a goal of cutting poverty in half over 10 years, which showed that mainstream Democrats were no longer on the defensive.

John Edwards sought to inject poverty into the agenda of the 2008 presidential election, and the ascent to the White House of an African American who had worked as an organizer in low-income communities, and whose campaign drew millions of poor Americans out of political quiescence, holds out the possibility that the conditions are right to once again "discover" poverty, as we do every few generations. While the economic crisis of the middle class has overshadowed much else, it has also made poverty a realistic worry for many who thought they were safely outside its grasp. The distinction between "the poor" and everyone else, or the deserving and undeserving poor, which reinforces the vicious polarization encouraged by politicians like Gramm, is no longer tenable. We are all in this together.

But even while poverty has been off the political agenda— perhaps even *because* it has been off the agenda—these have been years of quiet experimentation and fresh thinking when it comes to poverty policy. For example:

- Strategies to help poor families build assets, both for long-term security and to take advantage of economic opportunity, expanded from vague academic dreams to full-fledged experiments supported by foundations and government. The federal Assets for Independence program has provided matching funds to over 43,000 participants over 10 years.

- Welfare reform coincided with an economic boom in the late 1990s, which gave states unprecedented financial resources to concentrate on helping former welfare recipients move into the labor market and stay there. But while labor-market participation was higher, wages for lower-income workers stagnated. Income for the bottom 20 percent of households rose 11 percent from 1979 to 2006, while the richest 1 percent made two and a half times what they earned 30 years ago.

- Federal and state improvements in child-support enforcement brought more cash into poor single-parent families. Policy-makers also realized that the economic circumstances of poor fathers not living with their children have a significant impact on the well-being of children and women. Projects to support fathers and increase their income enjoyed support from the left and right as well as particularly strong support among African American leaders, including the current president.

- A concerted national effort to reduce teen pregnancy and childbearing led to significant progress during the 1990s. Teen pregnancy was reduced by 38 percent, and the birth rate for teens dropped by a third in that time. But in 2005, the rates began to creep back up, signaling a failure, at least in part, of the Bush administration's abstinence-only programs.

- By expanding eligibility for the Earned Income Tax Credit, Medicaid, and other safety-net programs, the basis of public benefit programs was shifted subtly from *need* to *work*. Conservative scholar Douglas Besharov warned in 2002 that this shift amounted to "a startling expansion of the welfare state" and that "new welfare" would be "bigger and, for its supporters, better than ever. It is billions of dollars and millions of recipients larger—and it enjoys much broader public support because it is tied to 'working families.'"

Meanwhile, however, parents without the ability or opportunity to work full time, year round faced more restrictions on their ability to pursue education and training. "New welfare" programs lifted 14 million people above the poverty line but were less effective at reducing deep poverty than were older programs, as shown by the rise in the number of children living below half the poverty line—2.4 million in 2005, a million more than a decade earlier.

As a result of these silent but dramatic shifts, we have a set of policies and circumstances relating to poverty and poor families that are as different from the policies of the late 1980s as those of the Great Society were from the decades previous. In many ways, these are policies designed to help people build their economic capacity when the economy is growing. They live up to the rhetorical calls for a "ladder" or a "trampoline"

More Than Welfare Is Needed to Reduce Poverty

[T]he drop in the poverty rate has not been as dramatic as the drop in the welfare rolls. Those who have left the rolls "we're finding in soup kitchens and shelters," said Sister of St. Joseph Mary Elizabeth Clark of NETWORK, a Catholic social justice lobby. "They're not making a living wage. They're not in a situation where their health care needs are met. They're trying to save on food so they can pay child care." . . .

Whether a person gets out of poverty is determined by more than simply welfare. The minimum wage, food stamps, health coverage and unemployment compensation are part of a long list of policies that affect whether people can make ends meet.

Teresa Malcolm, "Welfare Reform: Reduce Poverty Not Just Caseloads, Activists Say," National Catholic Reporter, March 1, 2002.

to replace the "safety net." Welfare reform, for example, was perceived as a great success in the economic boom of the late 1990s. But we shouldn't design anti-poverty policies for good times, when poverty is a relatively small problem in the midst of affluence, but for times when they will be put to the test by rising economic hardship. And the current economic crisis will provide a strenuous natural test of these newer initiatives.

As Alan Jenkins writes in this report, the federal response to the severe recession—the economic stimulus package enacted in February—included a surprising array of little-noticed provisions to expand economic opportunity. While much work needs to be done to ensure that this reinvestment actually boosts the economic capacity of those left behind even in good times, it has been decades since the federal government moved so aggressively to extend economic opportunity to the poor.

But money and economic opportunity are not the only answers to poverty. We have come a long way from the days when John F. Kennedy's economic adviser, Walter Heller, could treat the problem as a matter of setting a poverty threshold and calculating how much money it would take to bring every poor household above it. It is no longer possible to deny that expectations, incentives, structural racism, neighborhood, schooling, family structure, and many other factors are deeply intertwined with poverty, particularly with its intergenerational cycle. But knowing that doesn't make it any easier to solve. In fact, the complexity of these intertwined factors, and the context of relentless economic disruptions, makes it far too complicated for anyone to start a sentence with "The key to reducing poverty is . . . ."

The last decade has brought tremendous experimentation to these complex questions, including successful initiatives toward asset-building; cash incentives to encourage good behavior; initiatives to encourage social, racial, and economic mobility and integration; interventions to rebuild community; and supports for the working poor and childless workers. Some or all of these initiatives, as they show success, should be brought to scale so that they reach more than one city, one community, or one subpopulation. The core of this special report will assess these initiatives, their successes and limitations, the potential choices to be made among them, and the steps that can be taken to deepen their impact.

The challenge is to develop a set of policies that are suitable to both good times and bad and that provide both opportunity to help poor people get into the mainstream of the economy and security against the harsh disruptions of that economy and of life in general.

Apart from finding the right mix of policies, it will be necessary to bring these new ideas out from behind the curtain and rejoin the political fight. There are limits to what can be achieved invisibly, through the subtle changes that created the work-based safety net or through the quick enactment of the economic stimulus. We may not be ready to declare a new national "War on Poverty" at a time when all Americans feel economically vulnerable, but prioritizing poverty reduction, even without the misleading "war" metaphor, is both necessary and a political challenge. Great Britain provides an example of how anti-poverty efforts have proved politically successful, in part by setting a measurable goal so that policies can be evaluated. The election of Barack Obama, along with the sense of solidarity and shared vulnerability created by the recession, may allow a political reframing of poverty as part of a broader vision of a new social contract.

"Support for such [anti-poverty] policies is driven by the understanding among public policy scholars that social welfare programs actually help to reduce *poverty, rather than to perpetuate it."*

Welfare Helps Reduce Poverty

Anthony DiMaggio

Anthony DiMaggio is an author and the editor of Media-ocracy. *In the following viewpoint, he suggests that the issue of poverty is consistently underreported by the US media, especially the effect it has on America's children. DiMaggio details a 2010 Urban Institute report that shows poverty is taking a dramatic toll on children and families. He concurs with the Institute's view that government welfare programs reduce poverty at a time when corporations and government officials have declared war on the working class and poor. DiMaggio cites racism and job loss as two major challenges faced by Americans in poverty, and adds that these problems are compounded by a prevailing attitude that government welfare programs aggravate, rather than alleviate, poverty and unemployment.*

Anthony DiMaggio, "Forgotten Casualties of the Recession," *Counterpunch*, July 7, 2010. Reproduced by permission of *Counterpunch*.

As you read, consider the following questions:

1. What percentage of American children live in poverty in 2010, according to DiMaggio?

2. What percentage of American children does DiMaggio indicate are food insecure?

3. How does DiMaggio define structural racism?

Consistently ignored in reporting on the economic crisis is the dramatic toll it's taking on America's children. The prevalence of poverty has expanded dramatically in light of growing unemployment, accompanied by state attacks on social welfare spending that benefits the disadvantaged. Child poverty grew nationally to a total of 22 percent of all children in 2010, an all time high for the last two decades, and an increase in five percent over the last four years. Half of the poor are now classified as in "extreme poverty"—described as living in families earning below 50 percent of the poverty line. The percent of children who are food insecure also increased to 18 percent in 2010. This growth translates into an additional 750,000 children nationwide who are malnourished.

Reliance on food stamps increased by 24 percent between August 2008 and August 2009, with the number of children benefitting them growing from nearly 30 million to 37 million. Some localities are suffering under even higher levels of poverty. Throughout Illinois, up to 1.5 million people were reliant upon food stamps as of June 2009—an increase of 22 percent from 2007. From 2000 to 2008, child poverty increased by 72 percent in Colorado. Overall, more than 30 states saw their reliance on food stamps increase between 2008 and 2009.

Child Poverty Is an Unexamined Problem

Sadly, attention to child poverty isn't considered "sexy" enough to make the headlines or features in the "paper of record" (*New York Times*) or other agenda setting media. A review of stories featuring child poverty from August 2008 (at the time of the economic meltdown) through June 2010 finds that the issue was only featured in a single *New York Times* story and just three stories in the *Washington Post*.

Recently released data from a 2010 panel study by the Urban Institute (covering the period from 1968 through 2005) finds that childhood poverty is likely to be perpetuated into adulthood among the disadvantaged. The nuances of child poverty and its perpetuation over time, however, are lost in a media culture that favors the instant gratification of daily updates on Lindsay Lohan's drug abuse over detailed coverage of national poverty. The media blackout on child poverty means that the causes of, and solutions to this phenomenon remain obscure to much of the public. The racial dimension of child poverty, for one, is left unaddressed. The Urban Institute reports that black children "are roughly 2.5 times more likely than white children to ever experience poverty and seven times more likely to be persistently poor . . . 31 percent of white children and 69 percent of black children who are poor at birth go on to spend at least half their childhoods living in poverty."

Conservative perspectives framing poverty as the result on personal laziness and due to the welfare state enabling dependency are also left unchallenged when the racial aspects of child poverty (and child poverty itself) are ignored in media. The Urban Institute reports that "those poor at birth are more likely to be poor between ages 25 and 30, drop out of high school, have a teen nonmarital birth, and have patchy employment records than those not poor at birth." Conservatives (and increasingly a fair amount of center-left liberals) will no doubt blame these problems on the "bad habits" developed by the poor throughout their lives and to personal laziness, but these positions ignore structural barriers in society that ensure the continuation of poverty.

Some Welfare Policies Are Especially Effective at Reducing Poverty

We find that more lenient eligibility requirements for welfare receipt and more generous financial incentives to work generally reduce deep poverty. . . . We also find that an increase in the vehicle amount exempt in determining a family's assets for eligibility purposes reduces deep poverty of children. On financial incentives to work, our results suggest that states' welfare benefit levels, sanction policies, treatment of child-support income, and minimum wage levels can be used to reduce deep poverty.

We find that the effect of eligibility requirements and financial incentives to work on poverty are somewhat mixed. . . . On financial incentives to work, our results suggest that more generous financial incentive to work policies lead to lower poverty rates in some cases and higher poverty rates in others. Specifically, we find that more generous state minimum wage and more lenient sanction duration policies reduce poverty, while higher benefit levels increase poverty. Higher benefit levels can lead to increased poverty if it leads individuals to reduce their labor supply.

Finally, our results suggest that some stricter time limit policies may decrease deep poverty and poverty rates. Specifically, two time limit policies—having an intermittent time limit and having no time limit exemption for an ill family member—are consistently found to affect deep poverty and poverty of mothers and children. . . . [S]trict time limits can decrease poverty if they encourage individuals to enter the labor force. . . .

Signe-Mary McKernan and Caroline Ratcliffe,
"The Effect of Specific Welfare Policies on Poverty,"
The Urban Institute, April 2006.

Acknowledging Obstacles to Progress

Structural racism—characterized by widespread residential and education segregation in the U.S.—is ignored in conservative and neoliberal propaganda against the poor. That poor school districts have been shown to systematically perform worse in academics than wealthier districts is ignored in conservative rhetoric, which claims that "throwing money at the problem" of underperforming schools "solves nothing." Historically racist practices such as redlining, which targets poor and minority residents of the inner city, have succeeded in keeping most of disadvantaged African Americans and Hispanics from moving into more prosperous urban and suburban communities, and from accessing school districts that benefit from greater resources, but are located in more affluent school districts.

Empirical studies from as recently as the 1990s onward also demonstrate that black applicants are systematically more likely to be discriminated against by being denied bank loans, even after taking into account the fact that blacks as a demographic group are more likely to be poor and have weaker credit records. In other words, racist institutions that discriminate in their determination of "creditworthiness" based on an applicant's skin color help to ensure the perpetuation of U.S. structural segregation and racism.

Protecting Corporate Interests

The lack of jobs in urban slums (which are disproportionately occupied by poor blacks and Hispanics) is a result of the movement of manufacturing jobs from cities to the suburbs, and then abroad. This loss of jobs is another major source of sustained racial inequality. Sadly, this reality is ignored in the obsession with personality-based explanations of poverty. The steady decline of the purchasing power of the minimum wage (since its height in the late 1960s) also ensures that the poor will continue to be poor, even when they find jobs and seek to

"get off welfare." Attempts to address the problem of low paying jobs are held with contempt by Republicans, conservatives,
and neoliberal Democrats who believe that corporations
shouldn't be the subject of regulations that limit their profit-
ability or raise the living standards of the masses.

Those responsible for studying poverty at the Urban Institute appear to understand these basic biases of American society—long ignored by those who hold the poor in contempt.
The institute supports government intervention as a means of
fighting poverty, including initiatives such as increased access
to education, job training, and work support (such as child
care payments to working parents). Support for such policies
is driven by the understanding among public policy scholars
that social welfare programs actually help to *reduce* poverty,
rather than to perpetuate it. The Urban Institute's analysis is a
breath of fresh air at a time when the social welfare state is in
decline and corporate America and government officials have
declared war on the working class and poor.

Periodical and Internet Sources Bibliography

The following articles have been selected to supplement the diverse views presented in this chapter.

Athens News	"The Impact of Welfare Reform in America," January 31, 2011.
Douglas J. Besharov	"End Welfare Lite as We Know It," *New York Times*, August 15, 2009.
Anthony B. Bradley	"Welfare Reform Is Working," Acton Institute, August 22, 2006.
Ron Haskins	"The 2010 Reauthorization of Welfare Reform Could Result in Important Changes," The Brookings Institution, December 18, 2009.
John Hood	"The Bipartisan Success of Welfare Reform," *Carolina Journal Online*, September 5, 2008.
Kay S. Hymowitz	"Welfare Reform Worth Celebrating," *Seattle Post-Intelligencer*, July 16, 2006.
Jeff Jacoby	"Welfare Reform Success," *Boston Globe*, September 13, 2006.
Robert Scheer	"Clinton's Blindness on Welfare Reform," *The Nation*, August 30, 2006.
Cat Sullivan	"Welfare Reform is Not a Success," *Seattle Post-Intelligencer*, August 29, 2006.
Michael D. Tanner	"The Critics Were Wrong: Welfare Reform Turns 10," *San Francisco Chronicle*, August 21, 2006.
Urban Institute	"A Decade of Welfare Reform: Facts and Figures," June 2006.
Richard Wolf	"How Welfare Reform Changed America," *USA Today*, July 18, 2006.

CHAPTER 2

How Has the Recession Affected Welfare?

Chapter Preface

One of the major legislative controversies of 2009 was the passing of the American Recovery and Reinvestment Act, also known as the Stimulus Act. The Act approved a government funded, $900 billion economic stimulus package that aimed to create jobs, fuel consumer spending, and promote investment during the sharp economic downturn that began in 2006–2007. It was thought that stimulus funds would help get the US economy moving in a positive direction—and, at the very least, prevent the country from slipping into an even more severe economic depression.

Critics roundly opposed the Stimulus Act, also referred to as the stimulus package, arguing that the spending in the bill would not make a significant difference in the country's economic situation. Others complained that the investment in infrastructure projects would take too long to create jobs and economic benefits. Many viewed the package as too much government spending and not enough tax cuts. Some believed that the stimulus package did not go far enough and wouldn't provide the right amount of stimulus to the ailing economy.

Another aspect of the Stimulus Act that garnered widespread and strong criticism was the creation of a $5 billion emergency fund to help states pay for added welfare recipients, known as the Temporary Assistance for Needy Families (TANF) Emergency Fund. Policymakers argued that emergency welfare funding was needed because many Americans were losing their jobs, homes, and savings during the recession and as a result, the number of people needing emergency assistance was climbing. Under TANF emergency funding, states that increased welfare assistance or subsidized employment received 80% reimbursement of these new costs. Moreover, the fund allocated $87 billion to subsidize state Medicaid costs; increased spending on food stamps by 12 percent; augmented funds for the federal school lunch program and the Women, Infants & Children (WIC) nutrition program; and provided tax cuts to low-income taxpayers.

Critics view the TANF Emergency Fund to be a stealthy undoing of 1996 welfare reform, which has remained a controversial act in the years since its implementation. Under the old welfare system, the federal government paid states for the number of people on the welfare rolls; when the number of people increased, so did the funding. Under welfare reform, the federal government provided block grants to the states to design and administer their own welfare systems. States enacted strict criteria on eligibility and time limits on how long families could receive welfare assistance. State policymakers also emphasized putting welfare recipients to work; cut benefits to young, unmarried parents; and rewarded marriage. With the TANF Emergency Fund, critics argued that the federal government was reversing the gains made with welfare reform by taking back the funding power from the states. Once again, critics pointed out, the federal government was rewarding states for increasing their welfare caseloads.

In March 2010 Republican Senators, along with a few Senate Democrats, blocked the reauthorization of the TANF Emergency Fund. With the program set to expire in September 2010, supporters maintained that a failure to renew the program would mean the loss of 240,000 jobs. A key component of the fund was that it subsidized jobs with private companies, nonprofits, and government agencies for the unemployed. Some policymakers proposed expanding the Fund, arguing that the economy's slow recovery and continued high unemployment signaled the need for even broader economic assistance for those who needed it.

Although the House of Representatives approved the extension of the program, the Senate continued to block it. The TANF Emergency Fund was allowed to expire on September

30, 2010. There have been numerous calls to reinstate the program, in spite of the political opposition to it.

This chapter explores how the recession has impacted welfare reform. Other topics examined are whether the Stimulus Act reverses welfare reform, the need for further welfare reform, and the necessity of a jobs program to help those who have been forced off of welfare.

> *"The undoing of welfare reform is par-*
> *ticularly difficult to stomach when con-*
> *sidering . . . important headway we*
> *were making to curb the danger of*
> *making free citizens dependent on gov-*
> *ernment."*

The Stimulus Bill Reverses Welfare Reform

Israel Ortega

Israel Ortega is a senior media services associate at the Heritage Foundation. In the following viewpoint, he finds that the most egregious part of the 2009 federal stimulus bill is the rollback of what he considers sensible bipartisan welfare policies that curbed dependency on government handouts. Ortega argues that the United States should not go back to what he characterizes as failed government policies that have hurt the country's most needy and vulnerable citizens.

As you read, consider the following questions:

1. What does Ortega state as the price tag for the 2009 stimulus bill?

Israel Ortega, "Rolling Back Welfare Reform," The Heritage Foundation, March 5, 2009. Reproduced by permission of The Heritage Foundation.

2. According to Ortega, what is the most expensive spending bill in US history?

3. How far did the poverty rate for children of single mothers fall between 1995 to 2004, according to statistics cited by Robert Rector and quoted by Ortega?

There are many disturbing features to the "stimulus" bill recently signed into law—its massive $787 billion price tag, the fact that it empowers a more intrusive and expansive government, its countless millions for wasteful pet projects.

But the repeal of many sensible welfare reform policies stands out as especially egregious. The bill could undo the bipartisan work of the last 15 years to curb government dependency. It could roll back one of the greatest legislative triumphs of our time.

In its haste to meet an arbitrary deadline, Congress voted on a massive, 1,000-plus page bill in the course of 48 hours. That's fast, especially by congressional standards. The stimulus bill is also the most expensive spending bill in our country's history. And with our country already facing record deficits, it's likely that our children and grandchildren will still be paying off the stimulus bill decades from now.

The Bill Is Political

As if the price tag and the amount of debt our country is leaving future generations weren't bad enough, the inability of so many of the bill's authors to resist injecting politics in the process is particularly disconcerting.

The rewriting of many of the 1996 welfare reforms perfectly illustrates how politicians are willing to attach unrelated provisions to any bill that's virtually guaranteed to be signed into law.

The undoing of welfare reform is particularly difficult to stomach when considering where we've been, and the impor-

A Trojan Horse

The fact that the stimulus proponents seek to conceal the bill's massive permanent changes in welfare is a clear indication that they understand how unpopular these changes would be if the public became aware of them. Far from an exercise in "unprecedented transparency"—as President Obama claims—the stimulus bills are an example of unprecedented deception.

Robert Rector and Kiki Bradley,
"Stimulus Bill Abolishes Welfare Reform and Adds New Welfare
Spending," The Heritage Foundation, February 11, 2009.

tant headway we were making to curb the danger of making free citizens dependent on government.

Ending Welfare Dependency

Beginning in the late 1960s, during President Lyndon Johnson's Great Society and his War on poverty, the federal government (under both Republican and Democratic administrations) has spent trillions of dollars trying to eradicate hunger and homelessness. Unfortunately, "you get what you pay for," and many of these programs—by paying people to remain on the dole—created incentives for many to remain poor and abuse the system.

Thus the federal government's War on poverty actually led to an increase in poverty, due in large part to a rise in divorce rates and out-of-wedlock births. Instead of encouraging people to work, the outdated and misguided welfare programs actually encouraged unwed mothers to have more children so they could receive bigger paychecks from Washington.

By the early 1990s, it was clear that dramatic changes were necessary to curb government dependency and encourage people to empower themselves by rejoining the workforce. As a step toward these goals, Democratic President Bill Clinton signed into law the Personal Responsibility and Work Opportunity Reconciliation Act (passed by a Republican Congress) in 1996 after years of hard work and negotiations.

Despite admonitions by many, the act proved a resounding success. According to congressional testimony in 2006 by my colleague Robert Rector (a key author of the legislation), "the poverty rate for children of single mothers fell at a dramatic rate of 50.3 percent from 1995 to 41.9 percent in 2004. And the explosive growth of out-of-wedlock childbearing has come to a near standstill."

Stimulus Bill Enact Failed Policies

Unfortunately, that progress is now at risk.

Tucked away in the massive "stimulus" bill is a provision that says, "the federal government will actually begin paying states bonuses to increase their welfare caseloads." This is precisely the sort of perverse incentive likely to prompt more people to enroll in welfare, taking us back to the bad old days of dependency.

There's little doubt we're facing difficult times. But we shouldn't turn to failed policies of the past that have done more to hurt than help America's most needy.

"*The TANF provisions of the new law are intended to ensure that states have the resources they need to avert serious hardship among very poor children and their parents as a result of the deepening recession.*"

The Stimulus Bill Does Not Reverse Welfare Reform

Sharon Parrott

Sharon Parrott was the director of the Welfare Reform and Income Support Division of the Center on Budget and Policy Priorities (CBPP). In the following viewpoint, she maintains that criticizing the Stimulus Bill (American Recovery and Reinvestment Act) for undercutting welfare reform is a mischaracterization of the provisions of the legislation. Parrott argues that such charges ignore the devastating economic effects the recession is having on many US families and that it is more important than ever to provide assistance to those suffering during a time of economic hardship. She outlines all of the ways in which the welfare provisions of the Stimulus Bill support the key components of welfare reform, and adds that they meet with the approval of the lead Republican staffers in charge of the 1996 welfare reform legislation.

Sharon Parrott, "Despite Critics' Overheated Rhetoric, the Economic Recovery Bill Does Not Undermine Welfare Reform," Center on Budget and Policy Priorities, February 17, 2009. Reproduced by permission of Center on Budget and Policy Priorities.

As you read, consider the following questions:

1. What percentage of the increase in expenditures will federal funding pay states to cover increased costs under the Stimulus Bill?

2. What is the first problem with the existing contingency fund, according to Parrott?

3. What does Parrott say is the second problem with the existing contingency fund?

The economic recovery legislation provides additional resources to states where more poor families need basic assistance due to the recession and the states have responded by serving more families in their TANF (Temporary Assistance for Needy Families) programs. TANF is the welfare-reform block grant that the 1996 welfare law established to replace the old welfare system.

Some critics, such as Robert Rector of the Heritage Foundation, have charged that the TANF provisions of the recovery legislation undermine welfare reform. This criticism mischaracterizes the TANF provisions in the legislation. It also ignores a basic reality—poverty and hardship are rising substantially as a result of the recession, and the number of poor children and families in need is increasing. Ron Haskins—the lead House Republican staffer on the 1996 welfare law—has called for the very type of TANF provisions the recovery legislation contains and has said such measures are fully consistent with the 1996 law.

What the New TANF Provision Does

The TANF provisions in the recovery legislation provide states with additional resources through an "emergency contingency fund" if their TANF caseloads—and, thus, the costs of providing basic assistance to needy families with children—have increased and the states have responded by boosting expenditures for such assistance. The provisions also provide additional resources to states that respond to rising need by expanding subsidized employment programs or programs that provide short-term, non-recurrent aid, such as to help families pay security deposits or avoid utility shut-offs. Under the new legislation, states experiencing increased costs in these areas, as compared to the costs they incurred in 2007 or 2008, will be able to receive federal funding to cover 80 percent of the increase in expenditures. States will have to pay the other 20 percent of the costs either by increasing state spending— which will be difficult given the large budget shortfalls states face—or by cutting TANF-related funding from other areas such as child care or child protective services to meet these rising costs.

The recovery legislation also includes a provision ensuring that the *percentage* of families receiving TANF assistance that a state must enroll in welfare-to-work programs will not automatically spike upward if a state's caseload rises during the recession. Under standard TANF rules, the "work participation rate" that a state must meet—that is, the share of adult TANF recipients who must be employed or in welfare-to-work activities—is reduced based on the extent to which the state's caseload has fallen *below* its 2005 level. This means that if a state's caseload increases during the current recession, the work participation rate that the state must meet automatically rises as well. The standard rules thus would trigger especially sharp increases during the recession in the number of parents a state must engage in welfare-to-work activities. This would be a difficult requirement for states to meet during a deep economic downturn, when job placement opportunities diminish rather than expand.

The new legislation addresses this problem; under it, states that experience caseload increases during the recession will not face an increase in their required work participation rate. *But they will have to increase the number (as distinguished from the percentage) of parents engaged in work activities, since the same work participation rate will now apply to a bigger caseload.* Without this aspect of the new legislation, a state experiencing modest increases in its caseload could be required to expand the size of its welfare-to-work program by 40 or 50 percent, a particularly difficult and expensive undertaking when jobs are scarce. (In normal economic times, a large share of TANF recipients who are in work activities are working in unsubsidized low-income jobs and receiving a TANF grant to supplement their earnings.)

Why the TANF Provisions of the Recovery Legislation Are Needed

The original 1996 welfare law included a "contingency fund" to provide states with additional resources during recessions. But there are two problems now with the existing contingency fund. First, it may well run out of money in 2009, as states draw down the available funding. Second, some states have been able to draw down funding because they have met the economic "triggers" for the fund, but then have not used the money to provide basic assistance to additional families in need.

To address these problems, the new legislation provides additional "emergency" contingency funds on a temporary basis and makes them available only to states that provide basic assistance to a larger number of families, expand subsidized employment, or expand programs providing short-term non-recurrent aid to needy families. This ensures that the funding is targeted on states where additional families that need assistance to make ends meet are receiving help.

Many analysts have voiced concern that in some states that are experiencing large increases in unemployment and corresponding increases in food stamp caseloads, the TANF program has not responded to the rise in poverty. Although TANF caseloads are increasing in some states, they remain flat or are declining in others where unemployment has increased substantially. The TANF provisions of the new law are intended to ensure that states have the resources they need to avert serious hardship among very poor children and their parents as a result of the deepening recession.

Addressing the Criticisms

The criticisms leveled against the TANF provisions of the legislation reflect both rhetorical excess and a lack of careful scrutiny of the provisions. These provisions do not undermine welfare reform. Nor do they undo its focus on work.

- *States will have no incentive to put families on TANF that don't need assistance.* Under the new provisions, states will have to find the resources to cover 20 percent of the additional costs associated with TANF caseload increases. States face cumulative budget deficits over the next 30 months estimated at $350 billion. The fiscal relief that the recovery legislation provides to states will close only about 40 percent of these shortfalls. States thus will have no incentive to push families who don't need TANF assistance onto the rolls, as that would increase the costs that hard-pressed states would have to bear.

- *The 1996 law itself established a contingency fund to be drawn upon in recessions—the new legislation simply ensures there is enough money available and that the new emergency contingency funds are targeted on states that need it.* The 1996 welfare law assumed states would need more resources when poverty increased during a recession. The new legislation adds some additional resources and targets the new funding to states facing increases in the number of families that need assistance and are receiving aid. Some critics have argued that states meeting certain economic triggers—such as increased unemployment rates—should have had access to the additional funding, even if they do not use the funding to cover the costs of aiding more poor families. But TANF was not intended to provide general fiscal relief to states. It is a funding stream intended to meet the needs of poor children and their families.

- *States experiencing caseload growth will be required to expand their work programs and place more parents into welfare-to-work activities.* Under the new legislation, a state that experiences caseload grow of 10 percent will have to increase the number of parents participating in welfare-to-work activities by 10 percent in order to meet the federal work participation requirements. The new provision simply ensures that states with ballooning deficits and weak job markets are not expected to increase the number of parents working or in job training programs by a substantially *larger* percentage than the percentage increase in their TANF caseloads.

- *Ron Haskins, the Republican staff director of the Ways and Means Subcommittee on Human Resources when the 1996 welfare reform law was written and a key figure in the crafting of that legislation, has said that TANF provisions like those the new legislation contains are needed now and are fully consistent with the 1996 welfare law.* In a recent memo (co-authored with the author of this analysis), Haskins wrote:

  > Currently, a state can draw down TANF contingency funds even if it is not serving more families in its TANF cash assistance program. . . . [T]he new contingency funds [in economic recovery legislation] . . . should be targeted to states that are assisting increasing numbers of families and are, therefore, facing increased costs. This policy change would return the contingency fund to its original purpose—helping

states that are assisting increasing numbers of families and are, therefore, facing increased costs. This policy change would return the contingency fund to its original purpose—helping states meet higher assistance costs during recessions—and show states that if they ensure that their program responds to rising need during the downturn, the federal government will help cover the cost.

> *"It would be wise to figure out who the program is really for: the states or their citizens?"*

Welfare Is Being Underutilized During the Recession

James Warren

James Warren is a reporter for Bloomberg News. *In the following viewpoint, he investigates the mystery of why many Americans who are eligible for welfare benefits are not taking them. Warren finds that states have implemented "diversion strategies" to keep eligible people from enrolling in the program in order to keep caseload numbers down. He suggests that although these practices might be good for the state's balance sheets, they are not good for the people who need help in tough economic times.*

As you read, consider the following questions:

1. How many Americans does Warren state were on welfare in 2008?

2. In what states did cash assistance drop between mid-2008 and mid-2009?

3. How many people eligible for welfare are not taking part, according to Warren?

James Warren, "The Mystery of Welfare and the Recession," *Bloomberg Businessweek*, May 20, 2010. Reproduced by permission.

Something doesn't compute about the historic welfare-to-work law backed by President Clinton and passed by a Republican-led Congress in 1996. As expected, the number of Americans on welfare has plummeted, from 4.8 million back then to around 1.7 million in 2008. Despite attempts to cast the law as a cold-blooded way to toss people off the dole, it was written—and funded—with knowledge that there would still be tough times. Thus, it set aside $2 billion in case an economic event might one day spark a rush to welfare. So why are caseloads still declining in states when there's little work to be had?

"It doesn't make sense," says Ron Haskins, who helped author the fundamental change in social policy as a staff director for the GOP majority on the House Ways & Means Committee. Unemployment is at 9.9% and nearly 40 million people are on food stamps. But between mid-2008 and mid-2009, as the recession took hold, New York, New Jersey, Michigan, and Texas were among states where cash assistance dropped, even as it rose sharply in Nevada, California, Colorado, and elsewhere. "We found no clear association between the change in the number of families receiving cash assistance in a state and its unemployment rate," said the Government Accountability Office after interviewing welfare officials in 21 states.

Welfare reform—or the Personal Responsibility & Work Opportunity Reconciliation Act of 1996—morphed the program from monthly cash payments to grants dependent on recipients seeking work via Temporary Assistance for Needy Families (TANF). The Health & Human Services Dept. administers TANF, with $16 billion budgeted annually for the states. HHS insists that states receiving funds make sure a minimum percentage of TANF recipients work a certain number of hours weekly and heed a lifetime limit of 60 months of aid. That may sound like a long time, though the program is not overly generous: A single mother of two gets less than $400 a month in assistance.

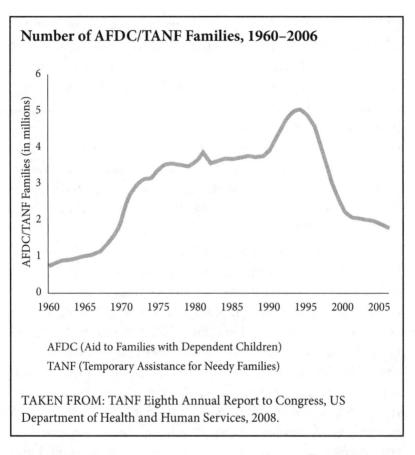

Number of AFDC/TANF Families, 1960–2006

AFDC (Aid to Families with Dependent Children)

TANF (Temporary Assistance for Needy Families)

TAKEN FROM: TANF Eighth Annual Report to Congress, US Department of Health and Human Services, 2008.

The extra $2 billion in funding was to ensure that states could take on more recipients during a recession. When it threatened to run out, the Obama Administration set aside an emergency $5 billion more. Yet "unemployment and the length of unemployment increases, and welfare rolls are merrily going down!" says Haskins, now the co-director of the Brookings Institution's Center on Children & Families. He can't make sense of it.

What we know is that more than 3 million people eligible for welfare are not taking part. According to the little-noticed GAO report, released in March, the reasons people are scared off include rules mandating job-related searches; declining cash benefits, which "have not been updated or kept pace with inflation"; and sanctions tied to the search process. Investigators also discovered state "diversion strategies" to keep applicants from staying on the program. States can steer applicants into taking a lump sum for, say, three months of assistance; then they're not counted on the state's regular TANF rolls or required to maintain contact with the welfare office. Says Larry Temple, executive director of the Texas Workforce Commission: "The paternalistic 'we know better' attitude is what got us into trouble. For some this is the best thing."

Perhaps, though there are other factors that indicate the choice may not be entirely up to the individual. For one thing, that $2 billion set-aside? Budget-strapped states have pilfered it to fund child-care programs and other measures that aren't actually welfare. There's also a perverse incentive to decrease the rolls. A state can drop the percentage of recipients who need to seek work if the state reduces the total caseload. Temple concedes there has not been "the uptick people thought we'd have" but says that's because Texas is more efficient than other states in finding jobs for TANF recipients. Texas currently has 45,000 people on TANF and 8.2 percent unemployment, compared with 220,893 people in the program and 5.6 percent unemployment in 1996.

The law has altered the public perception of welfare and the culture of state administrators. It has been a sign of weakness to have caseloads go up, meaning new state welfare chiefs, like Jennifer Hrycyna in Illinois, confront not only their staffs' reflex to deny benefits but also the challenge of easing onerous rules. Instead of a family of three needing to earn less than $6,000 a year to be eligible in Illinois, the ceiling will soon be $9,000. "Work requirements should be structured to provide meaningful opportunities to recipients that will lead them toward long-term self-sufficiency," says Hrycyna, "rather than pushing people into unstable low-wage jobs that get families off the rolls but leave them in poverty." Congress will have to reauthorize the welfare act next year. It would be wise to figure out who the program is really for: the states or their citizens?

"True welfare should help everyone: the taxpayer, who is allowed to keep more of his or her paycheck, and the welfare recipient, who is lifted off the dole and up to independence."

Renewing and Expanding the TANF Emergency Fund Reverses Welfare Reform

Rachel Sheffield

Rachel Sheffield is a research assistant at the Heritage Foundation. In the following viewpoint, she asserts that the 2010 proposed increased funding of the Temporary Assistance for Needy Families (TANF) program will lead to dramatic increases in welfare caseloads, essentially reversing welfare reforms. Sheffield argues that 1996 reforms allowed emergency funds to be used in times of recession, and that an expansion of funding will only function to repeal reforms and recycle unsuccessful welfare policies.

Rachel Sheffield, "The Obama Budget: Expanding the Welfare State and Undermining Marriage," Townhall.com, March 19, 2010. Reproduced by permission of The Heritage Foundation.

As you read, consider the following questions:

1. How much money does President Obama propose to expand TANF in his 2010 budget?

2. What does Sheffield assert that Jim McDermott has proposed to expand the welfare system?

3. What is the Healthy Marriage grant program?

President Obama's 2010 budget outlines a plan to pay states to grow their welfare roles and eliminate efforts to fight family breakdown in low-income communities. Despite the fact that low work hours and fatherlessness are two of the greatest contributors to poverty in the United States, the newly released budget provides incentives for states to increase the size of their caseloads and also wipes out funding for healthy marriage programs that aim to decrease the number of children growing up in single-parent homes.

Prior to 1996, the federal government increased a state's welfare money as that state increased its caseload. Not surprisingly, this provided little motivation to help welfare recipients move into the workforce. The 1996 welfare reforms did away with this negative incentive and created the Temporary Assistance for Needy Families (TANF) program, leading to dramatic caseload declines and a decrease in the child poverty rate.

Unfortunately, these successful reforms were undercut in a variety of policy moves and all but wiped out by last year's stimulus bill that created the $5 billion TANF Emergency Fund. Once again, states are being paid to increase their caseload (80 cents on the dollar for every new case they receive beyond their numbers for 2007 or 2008).

Another Increase Signals More Welfare Caseloads

Now [March 2010] President Obama is proposing $2.5 billion more to extend this supposedly temporary emergency fund.

Stimulus Bill Reverses Welfare Reform Gains

With the passage of the so-called economic stimulus bill designed by the Democrat-run Congress and promoted by President Obama, the perverse incentives that actually reward states for enrolling and keeping people on the public dole are baaack! . . .

Unfortunately, the education and work requirements, which always had big loopholes, will go by the boards because the incentives for states to move people from welfare to work are gone.

Jane Chastain,
"The President's Plan to Stimulate Poverty,"
WorldNetDaily.com, February 26, 2009.

Although the President links the need for this emergency money to the current recession, the truth is that the 1996 welfare reform includes a $2 billion nest egg for tough economic times such as this. (And lest it be forgotten, the government already increased welfare spending for FY 2010 by $174.6 billion.) Moreover, the new funding would not even be dispensed to states based on their unemployment rates but merely doled out based on the size of their caseload.

Unfortunately, Rep. Jim McDermott (D-WA) has jumped on the bandwagon, proposing an even greater expansion to the welfare system. His legislation would allow states to collect as much federal money as needed to support their growing caseload (provided that the state does not receive more than 50 percent of its annual TANF dollars). The cost of this would dwarf the President's $2.5 billion request. Both Obama and McDermott are sending a clear message to states: increase your welfare rolls and you will be rewarded handsomely by the federal taxpayer.

Not only does the President plan to expand welfare, but he has also eliminated a program that aims to reduce the prevalence of single motherhood, one of the greatest contributors to poverty in the United States. The Healthy Marriage grant program provides help to those from low-income communities to learn skills for building strong marriages. To replace this program, President Obama has introduced his "Fatherhood, Marriage, and Families Innovation Fund." While this sounds similar in name, it is in fact just another jobs program, focused very little on fatherhood, marriage, or families.

The 1996 welfare reform encouraged individual liberty, promoting work and freedom from government dependence. Now, the current administration is moving backwards and pulling its most vulnerable citizens with it. True welfare should help everyone: the taxpayer, who is allowed to keep more of his or her paycheck, and the welfare recipient, who is lifted off the dole and up to independence.

> "Allowing [TANF] to expire means . . .
> throwing hundreds of thousands back
> into joblessness at the very moment we
> need to put America back to work."

The TANF Emergency
Fund Creates Jobs and
Should Be Reauthorized

Christine L. Owens and George Wentworth

Christine L. Owens is the executive director of the National Employment Law Project (NELP) and George Wentworth is a senior staff attorney at the same organization. In the following viewpoints, they underscore how successful the Temporary Assistance to Needy Families (TANF) Emergency Fund has been in creating jobs across the country. Owens and Wentworth argue that TANF's effectiveness should ensure its reauthorization, especially during the job crisis the United States is facing in recent times. They also point out the widespread and strong support TANF has with politicians and policymakers.

As you read, consider the following questions:

1. What percentage of Americans are "long-term unemployed," according to the authors?

Christine L. Owens and George Wentworth, "It's Not a Recovery Without Jobs," *Politico*, September 28, 2010. Reproduced by permission of National Employment Law Project.

2. How many jobs do the authors argue that TANF has created across the nation?

3. How does TANF encourage job growth, according to the authors?

Today's jobs crisis is a national emergency. Companies still aren't hiring, despite rebounding profits and a record $1.8 trillion in corporate assets. Private-sector employers have added only about 750,000 jobs this year [2010]—less than 9 percent of the 8.5 million lost during 2008 and 2009.

The unemployment rate has now topped 9 percent for 15 consecutive months. Roughly 15 million Americans are officially unemployed, and almost 9 million want full-time work but can only get part time.

Unemployment Remains a Crisis

The only time in the past 60 years that unemployment was so severe was during the 1981–82 recession. But even when unemployment was at its highest then, only about one in four unemployed workers was "long-term unemployed"—jobless for more than six months. Today, 42 percent are. More alarming, 23 percent have been jobless more than a year.

The "jobless recovery," in other words, remains a crisis for millions of unemployed workers.

But because companies are holding onto cash instead of creating jobs, government must do more to foster employment opportunities. Shockingly, however, Congress is on the verge of doing just the opposite.

The Need for TANF

On Thursday [September 30] one of the most successful job-generating provisions of the recovery act, the Temporary Assistance for Needy Families [TANF] Emergency Fund, is scheduled to expire. If it does, state programs that created nearly

250,000 jobs across the nation will likely disappear—almost overnight. The Senate needs to reauthorize this program, immediately.

Support for the program is widespread and crosses political lines. Mayors of big cities like Philadelphia, Providence, R.I., and San Francisco, as well as governors in large and small states agree that this is a stimulus program that succeeds in creating jobs.

The TANF Emergency Fund helps states encourage private hiring by reimbursing 80 percent of the costs of subsidizing new employment. The program targets low-income workers with children but is not limited to those receiving temporary assistance benefits. Thirty-five states have drawn more than a billion dollars from the fund, opening employment doors for a quarter-million Americans—including adults and some young people hired through summer youth programs.

The program has bipartisan support in the states. Mississippi's Gov. Haley Barbour, for example, hailed his state's program, STEPS, for "spur[ring] job creation in the private sector by assisting business owners with the upfront costs of hiring new workers." In just nine months, the STEPS program of gradually decreasing wage subsidies has placed more than 3,200 workers in private-sector jobs. Early results show that nearly all program completers have become permanent employees.

Meanwhile, the Put Illinois to Work program has found jobs paying $10 per hour for more than 27,000 unemployed individuals.

Jobs Programs Have Had Success

One key to the program's success is the flexibility it offers. Some states favor subsidies for jobs most likely to become full-time unsubsidized employment, while others focus on getting large numbers of the unemployed back to work as quickly as possible—even if the jobs may not become perma-

TANF and Jobs

As of April 1 [2010], some 26 states had been authorized to use TANF Emergency Funds to establish new or expand subsidized employment programs. Several additional states plan to begin operating such programs shortly. These states have plans in place to provide subsidized jobs to about 160,000 individuals by the end of September. In addition, 39 states have received TANF Emergency Funds to provide either basic cash support or non-recurring, short-term assistance to the growing number of very poor families with children. These families spend quickly any funds they receive, so this assistance helps sustain local merchants and, through them, neighborhood economies.

Liz Schott and LaDonna Pavetti,
"Extending the TANF Emergency Fund Would
Create and Preserve Jobs Quickly and Efficiently,"
Center on Budget and Policy Priorities, April 6, 2010.

nent. Many states have effectively become job-creation laboratories and customize solutions to fit local labor markets.

Despite this promising success, states are being forced to wind these programs down because the emergency fund expires on Sept. 30 [2010]. Congress can reverse this, clearing the way to put hundreds of thousands of low-income workers back to work by renewing the fund.

In fact, the state jobs programs nurtured through the emergency fund could easily form the foundation for a more expansive and aggressive response to the national jobs crisis—one that helps all categories of unemployed workers.

In today's job market, competition for any job squeezes out the undereducated, the overqualified and, quite often, applicants with long bouts of unemployment. That reality requires us to open as many doors into the labor market as possible—and as soon as possible.

Sustaining and Creating Job Opportunities

Whether providing opportunity for a teenaged cashier lacking other marketable skills or a downsized corporate worker with 30 years of experience, successful programs that encourage employers to reinvest in human capital must be supported.

As described in our recent report, "Where the Jobs Are," building a sustainable recovery ultimately requires good jobs that support families and communities. But to get there from here, we must extend a hand to the long-term unemployed through real opportunities.

Renewing the TANF Emergency Fund would be an important step in that direction.

Allowing it to expire means killing jobs when we should be saving them, throwing hundreds of thousands back into joblessness at the very moment we need to put America back to work.

> "Far from encouraging self-reliance, the welfare state's unrestrained growth spurt will force millions more into dependency on government."

Another Round of Welfare Reform Is Needed Now

Chuck Donovan and Robert Rector

Robert Rector and Charles A. Donovan are senior research fellows at the Heritage Foundation. In the following viewpoint, they contend that Congress must act to curtail what they characterize as an explosion of recent spending on welfare programs. Instead Congress must enact what they regard as proven reforms such as incentives for the unemployed to find jobs. Rector and Donovan also cite marriage promotion as a worthy goal of another round of welfare reform.

As you read, consider the following questions:

1. How much is the Obama administration planning to spend on six dozen means-tested welfare programs over the next decade according to the authors?

2. How much money do the authors say will be spent on welfare programs in 2011?

3. How many people do Donovan and Rector contend have moved off the welfare rolls and into jobs in the past 12 years?

To hear Washington politicians tell it, welfare reform is something they've already checked off their "to do" list. Been there and done that back in the '90s, veteran members of Congress boast.

So why would lawmakers even think about accepting the Obama administration's plans to spend $10.3 trillion on six dozen means-tested welfare programs over the next decade? Next year [2011] alone, welfare spending (cash, food, housing and medical care for the poor) is set to exceed $950 billion. For every $10 President Bush spent on welfare in 2008, President Obama expects to spend about $13. Far from encouraging self-reliance, the welfare state's unrestrained growth spurt will force millions more into dependency on government.

And, unless Congress acts, it will drive the nation into bankruptcy.

Investing in the American Dream

Instead, lawmakers should focus on proven reforms, including incentives for able-bodied adults to get jobs, for poor Americans with children to marry, and for states to contain costs and trim welfare rolls. While we're at it, why not give the poor a greater stake in realizing the American dream? We can do that by treating some welfare benefits as loans to be repaid, at least in part.

This approach also would rescue the able-bodied poor from a clear moral hazard. Right now, they're passive beneficiaries as government compels their fellow citizens, the taxpayers, to make outright grants with minimal expectations attached. A gift is good, but a reciprocal obligation would restore dignity and build character. After all, most of us are more likely to act responsibly when our own money is on the line.

These were among the principles Congress applied 14 years ago in voting to reform a significant portion of the fast-growing welfare system.

President Clinton signed the reforms into law in 1996, promising they would "end welfare as we know it." Congress replaced a failing program, Aid to Families with Dependent Children, with a new model called Temporary Assistance for Needy Families [TANF]. Under TANF, the federal government no longer sent blank checks for program managers to pass along. Instead, the law expected bureaucrats to control costs. And, in exchange for cash benefits, it required healthy adults to devote 20 to 30 hours a week to working or preparing for a job.

Within 12 years, we saw dramatic results: 2.8 million Americans, well over half the national caseload, moved off the welfare rolls and into jobs. Many of them were single mothers.

Welfare Spending Has Increased

But a funny thing happened on the way to ending welfare as we know it.

Adjusting for inflation, total welfare spending has nearly doubled since 1996. In a major shortcoming, Congress reformed only one of the 70 means-tested welfare programs. And in the past two years, even the gains under TANF came to a screeching halt. President Obama's economic "stimulus" package quietly created a $5 billion "emergency" fund. Bureaucrats used it to reward states where welfare rolls are growing again. Not even one in five of these "emergency" dollars goes directly to employment strategies.

Congress should insist that program managers enforce TANF's work requirements, and vote to extend them to other welfare programs such as food stamps and housing assistance.

Promote Marriage and Work Incentives to Reduce Welfare Dependence

Advocates for the poor have too long argued that welfare was the solution to poverty. Yet most evidence points in a different direction. The reform of welfare in 1996 has had far more positive effects on employment, earnings, and poverty rates than almost anyone anticipated. The data summarized in this brief suggest this is because work is a powerful antidote to poverty and that, in its absence, no politically feasible amount of welfare can fill the gap as effectively.

The short-term implication of this finding is that fiscally strapped states need help if they are to continue to fund programs that move welfare recipients into the work force and keep them there in a softer economy. The longer-term implication is that steps should be taken to move the entire system of benefits targeted to lower-income Americans more toward encouraging work and marriage and less toward providing unconditional assistance to those who do not work and who bear children outside of marriage. Because work-related benefits are more politically popular than those not tied to work, the system would not only be more effective per dollar spent, but it might well enjoy the political support that would make it more generous than the one it replaced.

Ron Haskins and Isabel Sawhill,
"Work and Marriage: The Way to End Poverty and Welfare,"
The Brookings Institution Policy Brief:
Welfare Reform and Beyond #28, September 2003.

Yes, the recession continues to leave too many Americans hurting and jobless. Once it ends, though, lawmakers should peel back total welfare spending to previous levels and cap future increases at the inflation rate. That alone would save $1.4 trillion.

Promoting Marriage Is Key

Promoting healthy marriage should be a centerpiece of welfare policy, as Congress envisioned. Because the child of a single mother is seven times more likely to live in poverty than the child of married parents, it's a national tragedy that four of every 10 babies are born to unmarried mothers. For blacks, the rate is seven in 10—a compelling reason for the Congressional Black Caucus to back real welfare reform.

Congress ought to address this crisis by reducing and eventually eliminating the "marriage penalty" that perversely strips benefits from Mom and Dad for being married and living together. One way: Increase the Earned Income Tax Credit for married couples. Congress also should direct welfare agencies to share the facts on marriage's benefits to residents of low-income neighborhoods. Here, especially, out-of-wedlock child-bearing—and thus poverty and a host of social ills—climbs ever higher.

With annual welfare spending closing in on $1 trillion—over four times the 1979 level, adjusting for inflation—it's time to reboot our anti-poverty programs to control costs and promote self-reliance. Work requirements and loans rather than giveaways are a solid start. If we as a nation also act to reverse the collapse of marriage, it'll be a wise investment in building strong working families and helping their children and communities prosper.

"POJ [Promise of a Job] . . . accepts as a basic assumption that the American people continue to support and require that anti-poverty efforts be based on work."

High Unemployment Necessitates Promise of a Job Program for Welfare-Leavers

Anthony J. Mallon and Guy V.G. Stevens

Anthony J. Mallon is a professor at Virginia Commonwealth University and Guy V.G. Stevens is a former senior economist with the Federal Reserve Board. In the following viewpoint, they call for the development and implementation of a new job creation program, Promise of a Job (POJ), that focuses on the millions of unemployed Americans who have left welfare since 1996. Mallon and Stevens believe that such a program is vital in order to address high levels of unemployment and create jobs. Mallon and Stevens envision POJ as not only a jobs creation program, but an anti-poverty program that is consistent with the work-first philosophy of welfare reform policies.

Anthony J. Mallon and Guy V.G. Stevens, "Promise of a Job: Reducing Poverty and Enhancing Children's Future Opportunity," *Spotlight on Poverty and Opportunity*, April 19, 2010. Reproduced by permission.

As you read, consider the following questions:

1. What is the HIRE Act as described by the authors?

2. How many million Americans had dropped out of the labor force or forced to work part time at the beginning of 2000, according to the authors?

3. According to POJ estimates cited by Mallon and Stevens, the plan will reduce the number of poor children by how many million?

With the unemployment rate persistently hovering near 10 percent for the past 8 months [August 2009–April 2010]—despite the recent and welcome job growth of 162,000 in March [2010]—national attention has increasingly, and rightfully, focused on the need to create jobs. On March 18 [2010], the President signed into law the HIRE Act, an $18 billion package of job-creation tax incentives and an additional $20 billion in direct spending on highway and transit programs. We applaud this effort but take the President at his word when he stated "While this jobs bill is absolutely necessary, it's by no means enough."

Further Action Is Essential

We concur because we are concerned that the HIRE Act and its predecessors will not adequately serve a key sub-group of the un- or underemployed: the millions of so-called welfare-leavers—Americans who have left TANF since 1996—more than half of whom find themselves mired in poverty. To address the special problems of welfare-leavers, we call for a job creation program, Promise of a Job (POJ).

While it has been widely publicized that TANF caseloads declined by 50 percent or more since the passage of the Personal Responsibility and Work Opportunity Reconciliation Act (PRWORA) in 1996, the high poverty rate of these welfare-leavers is much less well known. A number of interlinked problems limit the extent to which leavers are able to maintain stable, long-term employment.

First is the well-documented impact of personal and structural "barriers to work"—e.g., low basic skills, learning disabilities, poor understanding of workplace norms, the physical and mental health problems of leavers and their families, lack of affordable health care, unreliable transportation, and housing problems.

Second is the economy's pervasive inability to generate a sufficient number of jobs to employ all of those who want and need to work, even during the 'full employment' era of the late 1990s. For example, when the overall unemployment rate fell to 4.1 percent and 5.7 million were officially unemployed at the beginning of 2000, there existed another 7.4 million who had either dropped out of the labor force or who where involuntarily forced to work part time.

Supply and Demand of Labor

These problems of both labor supply and demand should come as no surprise. At the dawn of welfare reform, in his 1996–97 lectures and subsequent book, *Work and Welfare*, Nobel laureate Robert Solow predicted that without a serious program of job creation for welfare-leavers, "the transformation of welfare into work is likely to be the transformation of welfare into unemployment and casual earnings so low as once to have been thought unacceptable for fellow citizens." Solow drew an important and obvious conclusion: ". . . an adequate number of jobs for displaced welfare recipients will have to be deliberately created, either through some version of public-service employment or through the extension of substantial special incentives to the private sector."

We believe POJ can do much to correct the failure of TANF as an anti-poverty program—a failure that we fear will be repeated by the Obama administration's job programs. POJ builds on the transitional jobs program concept and is consistent with the work-first philosophy of TANF, but is also designed to be an anti-poverty program. POJ includes elements that address the difficulty for welfare-leavers to secure and *maintain* private-sector employment.

As an anti-poverty program, the wages of the jobs developed by the program will be sufficient, when combined with the EITC and Food Stamps, to lift the vast majority of participating families out of poverty. Adequate work hours will be assured by a job guarantee for a job in the public or private sector. POJ is described and costed-out in detail in some of our recent work, but we give a sketch of its components and costs below.

What Is POJ?

A general description of POJ includes four key components:

I. Recruitment/Referral

II. Assessment, Job Readiness Training, Job Development, Search and Placement

III. The Job

IV. Services after the Initial Placement: Monitoring, Mediation, Retention, and Entry into an Unsubsidized Job

The Recruitment/Referral Phase can be administered in cooperation with local TANF programs and make use of the existing workforce development infrastructure such as "One-Stop" centers. The goal of phase I is to prepare entrants and move them to jobs—preferably unsubsidized in the private sector, but, if necessary, subsidized positions with the public sector. What little firm evidence is available indicates that despite the many activities encompassed under this phase, the "work first" principle should be the guide. As stated by Charles Michalopoulos, Senior Fellow with MDRC, "The group of programs with the most consistent effects on employment and earnings were employment-focused programs that allowed some welfare recipients to enroll in short-term education or training."

The transitional job programs on which we based our phases II and III have shown quite impressive results in placing participants in full-time jobs, easily beating the 60 percent mark for TANF leavers through 2000 reported by the Department of Health and Human Services. If a subsidized position is required, we would recommend a job that requires a minimum of 30 hours of work per week, supplemented by an additional 10 paid hours for continued job searching and training to resolve remaining barriers to employment. As discussed in detail by the National League of Cities' Clifford Johnson when he was with the Center on Budget and Policy Priorities, a rich body of results and experience exists for subsidized transitional jobs in the private sector, local governments, public schools and non-profits.

However, despite the success of transitional job programs in initial job placements, many graduates have not remained fully or even satisfactorily employed one or two years after their initial placement. Phase IV, for post-employment monitoring and retention services, is our attempt to implement services provided in the few transitional job programs that have had relatively good results in maintaining full-time employment. The other part of the attempt to maintain employment is the job guarantee.

Costs Associated with POJ

In our other work in this area, using data from past transitional job programs, we estimate the annual costs for a single participant in POJ. The maximum cost for someone who uses all services, including a full-time minimum wage job (at $7.25/hour), would be between $17,100 and $19,360; for a participant graduating immediately into a non-subsidized job, the cost could fall by as much as $14,000. The overall gross costs

105

Employment Is Down and Returns to Welfare Are Up

The percentage of recent leavers working and not receiving TANF in 2002 is significantly lower than the percentage of early leavers working and not receiving TANF in 1999: 42.2 percent compared with 49.9 percent. Interestingly, there was little difference in the percentage that reported they had left welfare for work: about half of each group. This suggests that recent leavers had greater difficulty keeping a job. . . . Lower employment rates and more returns to TANF are consistent with a weaker job market. Employment is more difficult to find and to keep, and for some families, unemployment is a precursor to a return to cash assistance.

Pamela J. Loprest,
"Fewer Welfare Leavers Employed in Weak Economy,"
The Urban Institute, August 21, 2003.

of the program would depend on the overall scale, the length of time each recruit spends in publicly-supported employment, and the degree to which employers are induced to cover a percentage of these costs.

In addition, costs will vary over time as participants graduate to private-sector jobs or exit without necessarily securing private sector employment, and as new and returning participants are added to the program.

In our study, we also estimate the total costs of a number of simulated programs. For example, using the adults in the 2007 TANF population as the basis of eligibility, under what we think are reasonable assumptions, POJ could service 715,000 cases for between $4.6 and $7.9 billion. A smaller pilot program would of course be much cheaper.

Offsetting the costs related to POJ are a potentially wide range of increased revenues and reduced indirect costs: revenues from the productive work of the participants; increased income taxes paid; the reduction or elimination of the TANF benefits the entrant was receiving; and a long list of possible social or third-party benefits. Some of these revenues and cost savings can in principle be captured by the agency administering POJ, thus lowering the total direct costs incurred by the program; all are relevant for calculating the net social benefit of POJ.

Social Benefits of POJ

The potentially large, but more difficult to capture, net social benefits include: (1) the reduction of the direct and indirect costs of physical and mental illnesses—savings that are likely because of a participant's exit from poverty and joblessness; (2) the health and other costs for children, as mentioned above (which, again, will be reduced by an exit from poverty); (3) the stimulatory effects on local communities and the larger economy by increasing the earned income of millions of families; and (4) the savings to society at large by the demonstrably lower rates of crime and incarceration resulting from the reduction in the poverty rate and the increase in employment. When we examined the estimates of such social benefits, their magnitude overwhelmed any estimate of the net private and social costs.

For example, in our simulations related to the 2007 TANF population, a calculation of the savings from reducing the number of children in poverty alone more than compensates for the cost of the whole program. That simulation shows a fairly modest reduction in the number of poor children by 1.6 million, lowering the children's poverty rate from 18 percent to 15.8 percent. However, using recent estimates by Georgetown professor Harry Holzer and his colleagues that children's poverty costs the United States a *minimum* of $500 billion a year, this 12 percent drop in the percentage of children who are poor would save the country $60 billion—*more than 7 times POJ's maximum cost.*

It turns out the reduction in poverty in the above simulation is small when compared with other simulations—for example, when considering the costs and benefits of having implemented POJ in 1996 at the advent of "welfare reform." The reason is that by 2007, a much smaller percentage of the poor, especially poor children, was covered by TANF than in 1996 or 1997. By 2007, only 19 percent of poor children were covered, whereas 54 percent were covered in 1996.

POJ Reduces Poverty and Creates Jobs

POJ is built as an extension and expansion of existing transitional job programs and accepts as a basic assumption that the American people continue to support and require that anti-poverty efforts be based on *work*. Thus, POJ is consistent with PRWORA in acknowledging "personal responsibility" as a key element. But it also requires what PRWORA, despite its title, does not: that responsibility goes both ways; that American society shoulders its own responsibility of the "reconciliation of work opportunities" with personal responsibility by guaranteeing the availability of a job to everyone willing and able to work. We believe that a program containing a carefully designed job guarantee will go far toward eliminating this inconsistency in PRWORA that has led to so much poverty among welfare-leavers.

The gross costs of POJ are not low, but we have shown that the net benefits can be vast. Given the relatively small size of POJ when compared with the 2009 stimulus and present plans for creating jobs, it would appear easy to embed our program within the larger effort. We are concerned, however, that current proposals seem to concentrate so exclusively on the recently unemployed that the population of welfare-leavers and their families will be forgotten—especially when *overall* unemployment returns to more politically acceptable levels.

Finally, let us not forget about another social benefit from POJ that has so far not been entered into our calculations: the benefit of living in a society where we *actually*, rather than just rhetorically, strive to reduce poverty among our most vulnerable members, our children.

Periodical and Internet Sources Bibliography

The following articles have been selected to supplement the diverse views presented in this chapter.

Gary Bauer	"Ending Welfare Reform," *Washington Times*, February 26, 2010.
Katherine Bradley	"Unreforming Welfare," *National Review Online*, March 4, 2010.
Kiki Bradley and Robert Rector	"How President Obama's Budget Will Demolish Welfare Reform," The Heritage Foundation, February 25, 2009.
Alissa Figueroa	"Private Sector Adds Jobs. You Helped. Really!" *Christian Science Monitor*, October 8, 2010.
Michael Gerson	"A Bad, Necessary Bill," *Washington Post*, February 18, 2009.
Olivia Golden and Sheila R. Zedlewski	"Reject Proposal to End Welfare," *The Press-Enterprise*, June 14, 2009.
Ron Haskins	"The Future of Welfare to Work," The Brookings Institution, December 9, 2009.
Star Parker	"Back on Uncle Sam's Plantation," Townhall.com, February 9, 2009.
Monica Potts	"Welfare Reform Squandered," *The American Prospect*, November 11, 2010.
Robert Rector	"Secretly Ending Welfare Reform," *Washington Times*, February 26, 2009.
Robert Rector and Chuck Donovan	"Confronting the Unsustainable Welfare State," The Heritage Foundation, June 30, 2010.
Phyllis Schlafly	"LBJ's Great Society on Steroids," WorldNetDaily.com, February 25, 2009.

CHAPTER 3

How Do Welfare Policies Affect Families?

Chapter Preface

The US food stamp program, officially known as the Supplemental Nutrition Assistance Program (SNAP), is a kind of federal assistance aimed at helping low- and no-income individuals and families purchase food. At one time, assistance was issued in the form of paper stamps or coupons in different denominations that recipients could redeem in stores for food products, including soft drinks and candy. In the late 1990s, paper was phased out in favor of debit cards, a system known as Electronic Benefit Transfer (EBT). The program is administered by the US Department of Agriculture, but the benefits are distributed at the state level.

In 1996 comprehensive welfare reform became law. Not only did it affect cash assistance programs like Aid to Dependent Families and Children (AFDC), it also drastically reformed SNAP as well. New rules set a cap on benefits, tightened eligibility for prospective recipients, and tied benefits to work programs or jobs. As a result of these tougher rules and criteria, the number of food stamp recipients plunged by the late 1990s. With the devastating economic crisis of the late 2000s, however, the trend reversed because the need for food stamps spiked.

In November 2010, a record 43.6 million Americans received food stamps, marking an increase of 14 percent over the previous year. In Washington, DC, and Mississippi, more than one-fifth of residents received food stamps. The program's popularity can be attributed to the much-needed economic assistance it gives to hungry individuals and families who are being pounded by the recent economic recession: the national average value of food stamp benefits per household is $275 per month, although it varies from state to state. According to US Department of Agriculture statistics, a family of four spends a minimum of $508 a month on food; that means for a family of four living at or slightly above the poverty level, they must spend about a fourth of their monthly income on food. For a family struggling to remain financially viable, food stamps are an attractive and invaluable government assistance program.

Many policymakers consider the escalating dependency on food stamps an unfortunate necessity in a time of economic recession. They acknowledge that food stamps provide vital assistance for families affected by high unemployment and economic instability. However, the rising need and use of food stamps also prompts criticism. Many point to concerns with fraud and abuse of the program. Others criticize the program from an ideological standpoint and are troubled that the increasing reliance on food stamps will perpetuate an attitude of laziness and dependence.

There is also an outcry over the cost of expanding the availability of food stamps. In 2010 the federal government spent an estimated $63.6 billion on the program, which was a sharp increase from the $34.6 billion spent in 2008. During a time of serious deficits and government spending, many questioned the ultimate value of an expensive program.

Debate surrounding the value of SNAP is one of the subjects examined in the following chapter, which considers how welfare programs affect families. Other topics discussed are the efficacy of pro-marriage welfare policies and the impact that welfare reform has had on single mothers and unwed parenting rates.

> *"Marriage augments income, helps adults accumulate wealth, reduces several leading health problems of adults and, in most cases, provides the best rearing environment for children."*

Pro-Marriage Welfare Policies Help Families

Ron Haskins

Ron Haskins is a senior fellow at the Brookings Institution. In the following viewpoint, he states that policies promoting marriage could be one of the most productive social investments by the government because marriage has a variety of economic and social benefits. Haskins argues that welfare reform has had a lot of success in decreasing government dependency, and now policymakers should turn to welfare reform to tackle social problems and encourage pro-family and pro-education outcomes. He contends that policies that provide incentives for fathers to work, economic benefits to married parents, child care benefits, and job training for unskilled workers are crucial for moving parents off of welfare and toward success.

Ron Haskins, "Welfare Reform, 10 Years Later," *Baltimore Sun*, August 20, 2006. Reproduced by permission of Ron Haskins.

As you read, consider the following questions:

1. What does the author cite as the successes of the 1996 welfare reform law?

2. How would a new earned income tax credit help single men, according to Haskins?

3. What does Haskins state that government, businesses, and junior colleges should do to help create skilled jobs in the local economy?

On its 10th anniversary, the 1996 welfare reform law is being widely recognized as a striking success. Passage of the law was followed by a rapid decline in welfare rolls, historic increases in employment by poor, single mothers leaving or avoiding welfare, and the first substantial decline in child poverty since the early 1970s. Poverty among black children and kids in female-headed households reached all-time lows.

But it would be a mistake to think the nation's greatest social problems have been solved. Welfare reform could wind up playing an important role in resolving these problems, but only if researchers, policy analysts and public officials pursue new solutions to old problems as aggressively as they pursued welfare reform. Three areas deserve attention:

Marriage Should Be Promoted

The first is promoting marriage and reducing nonmarital births, which, thanks in part to initiatives by Congress and the Bush administration, are already major goals of the nation's social policy. Marriage augments income, helps adults accumulate wealth, reduces several leading health problems of adults and, in most cases, provides the best rearing environment for children. This means that promoting marriage could become the single most productive social investment by government.

We are in the beginning stages of a nationwide campaign to promote and strengthen marriage by mobilizing churches and other community groups. This movement would be stronger if federal and state governments change their tax and benefit laws to reduce marriage disincentives and fund local organizations engaged in pro-marriage activities.

Men Should Be Supported

A second problem is that far too many young males quit school, drop out of the labor force, commit crimes and live apart from and fail to support their children. Increased marriage rates would almost certainly have an effect because a commitment to wives and children provides the motivation and environment that discourage street culture and increase work and responsible behavior. Other community-run programs, especially those that provide mentoring, may have some effect in helping young males stay in school and find work.

Perhaps the most intriguing idea discussed by policy analysts is to provide a large incentive for men to work. Under current law, mothers receive up to $4,500 in supplemental cash through the Earned Income Tax Credit, are at least partially covered by health insurance, have access to food stamps, and often receive child care or access to Head Start. But men usually only receive food stamps.

With government relentlessly pursuing fathers to support their children, many poor dads are driven underground because a major portion of their legitimate earnings is deducted for support payments.

This unfortunate situation could be corrected by creating a new earned income tax credit for single men. As proposed by social policy researcher Gordon Berlin in a forthcoming paper, men who work at least 30 hours weekly would qualify for up to $4,500 in cash earnings supplements. This policy would convert a typical $6-per-hour job into an $8-per-hour job that might make young men reevaluate their interest in low-wage work. A mother and father working full time at $7-

Provisional Number of Marriages and Marriage Rate: United States, 2000–2007

Year	Marriages	Population	Rate per 1,000 total population
2007	2,197,000	302,226,000	7.3
2006[1]	2,193,000	294,527,000	7.4
2005	2,249,000	296,497,000	7.6
2004	2,279,000	293,623,000	7.8
2003	2,245,000	291,384,000	7.7
2002	2,290,000	288,369,000	7.9
2001	2,326,000	285,318,000	8.2
2000	2,315,000	281,422,000	8.2

[1]Excludes data for Louisiana.

Note: Populations are consistent with the 2000 census.

TAKEN FROM: National Center for Health Statistics, CDC.

per-hour jobs, which are widely available, could have combined income of more than $25,000 in earnings and an additional $8,000 from their combined tax credits. Their total income of $34,000 would put them within striking distance of the middle class.

Education and Training Are Needed

The third problem is education and training for the working poor. For the foreseeable future, the U.S. school system will produce a million or so dropouts every year. Many of these unskilled young people will eventually work in low-paying jobs.

The 1996 welfare law emphasized work over education because academic programs for school dropouts and others with low skills have a poor track record. But with so many former welfare mothers employed in low-wage jobs, many of them have a new understanding of the importance of training.

Government, businesses and junior colleges should develop training programs of a year or less that would lead to skilled jobs in the local economy. Many parents stuck in low-wage jobs would enroll in these courses, particularly if they receive help with child care and transportation. This approach is greatly preferable to mandating a living wage or other policies that impose burdens on employers.

The achievements of the 1996 welfare reform law, combined with generous, public work supports for mothers, are now sending a strong signal from government that welfare dependency must be replaced by employment. The success of this agenda opens new opportunities for government, working with the private sector, to intelligently address some of the nation's leading domestic problems.

Now is not the time to simply cite the considerable success of welfare reform without taking vigorous public and private action to attack the serious social problems that remain.

"Policies designed to shape, rather than respond to, family structure are unlikely to substantially reduce poverty, even in the long run."

Pro-Marriage Welfare Policies Do Not Help Families

Maria Cancian, Daniel R. Meyer, and Deborah Reed

Maria Cancian is an author and Professor of Public Affairs and Social Work at the University of Wisconsin-Madison; Daniel R. Meyer is also a Professor of Public Affairs and Social Work at the University of Wisconsin-Madison; and Deborah Reed is an author, researcher, and senior fellow at Mathematica Policy Research. In the following viewpoint, they acknowledge that poor, single-parent families are more vulnerable to economic downturns than two-parent families, but contend that there is little evidence that pro-marriage policies substantially reduce poverty. Cancian, Meyer, and Reed emphasize that the provisions included in the American Recovery and Reinvestment Act that emphasize supportive services for parents, such as childcare expenses, tax credits, and unemployment benefit expansion, are

Maria Cancian, Daniel R. Meyer, and Deborah Reed, "Promising Antipoverty Strategies for Families," The Urban Institute, April 2, 2010. Reproduced by permission of The Urban Institute.

essential, and that further expansion of such assistance programs, including health care coverage, is a worthy focus for future research and evaluation.

As you read, consider the following questions:

1. What percentage of American children were born to unmarried mothers in 2007, according to the authors?

2. What do the authors state were the median earnings for black and Hispanic men in 2007?

3. What were the median earnings for Hispanic and black women in 2007 as stated by the authors?

A large percentage of poor children live with just one parent, usually their mother, and single-parent families are more vulnerable to economic downturns than are two-parent families. Living arrangements also affect the optimal design of policies related to income support and child support. In this paper, we briefly review changes in family structure, the relationship between family structure and employment, and early evidence on differential impacts of the recession on families.

We then focus on policies that are essential to reducing poverty in the context of the current work-based safety net, in which low-income families with children rely increasingly on mothers' earnings. We argue that economically vulnerable families will benefit the most from policies that support resident parents' efforts to balance work and caretaking, and that support and enforce nonresident parents' contributions.

The recent changes in the American Recovery and Reinvestment Act (ARRA) are an important starting point for antipoverty policy supporting families, but most were time limited. While the recession highlighted the urgency of many of these programs, the needs they address are longstanding and require a sustained response.

Family Composition Has Changed

Children Are Less Likely to Live in Families with Both Parents and More Likely to Rely on Their Mothers' Earnings to Avoid Poverty

The American family has changed dramatically in recent decades, creating both challenges and opportunities for anti-poverty policies. The growing proportion of children raised in single-mother families means more children are at increased risk of economic deprivation, while the related increase in mothers' work and earnings have helped more children avoid poverty.

Decisions about marriage, childbearing, and work are increasingly disconnected. Forty percent of children were born to unmarried mothers in 2007; while their parents are often romantically involved at the time of the birth, most nonmarital relationships do not last. Further, many children born to married parents will see their parents divorce before the children turn 16. Thus, the majority of American children will live at least some part of their childhood in a family that does not include both biological parents.

While children are increasingly likely to experience family disruption, the growth in employment among married and unmarried mothers has altered the consequences of family structure for children's access to resources. Fewer children have a parent at home full time, regardless of family structure. Over two-thirds of married women with preschool-age children worked during 2006. Low-wage workers—even in married-couple families—face particularly difficult choices in balancing their responsibilities as parents and workers. At the same time, single mothers are increasingly likely to work, shouldering the primary responsibility for providing both care and financial support for their children. Coinciding with the implementation of the 1996 federal welfare reform, employment rates for single mothers increased substantially; over three-quarters of single mothers of preschool-age children now work for pay at least part of the year.

Child Poverty Remains High

In the current policy context, with very limited cash income supports available to nonworkers, poverty status largely depends on the number of working adults in the household, their hours of work and wage rates, and the number of children (and adults) they have to support. Declines in marriage have reduced the number of adults directly available to support the children, but declines in the number of children per woman have reduced resource needs, and increases in mothers' work have increased resources. Overall, the combination of these trends means that poverty rates for children have grown since the late 1960s and remain stubbornly high.

Earnings declines for less-educated men and the persistently lower average earnings of women have made it harder for families to make ends meet. Even though the earnings of men with low education have fallen in recent decades in absolute terms, and relative to women, male earnings remain higher than female earnings on average. More specifically, in 2007, the median earnings for employed high school graduates (without college educations) were about $33,000 (in 2008 dollars) for white men and $27,000 for black and Hispanic men; they were $21,000 for white and Hispanic women and $19,000 for black women. Thus, single-mother families are at a disadvantage both because they are more likely to have only one potential worker, and because of the relatively lower wages of women.

Pro-Marriage Policies Do Not Reduce Poverty

There Is Little Evidence That Policies Designed to Reduce the Proportion of Children Living in Single-Parent Families Can Substantially Reduce Poverty and Economic Distress

Children born to unmarried parents are at greater risk of poverty, and, . . . complex families resulting from births across multiple partners present particular challenges. We have outlined some strategies for responding to changes in family forms, but some would argue that these efforts amount to treating the symptoms rather than the underlying causes. To some extent, our approach reflects the need to respond to the current reality: 40 percent of U.S. children are born to unmarried parents, many or most of whom will have children with multiple partners. It also reflects our assessment that policies designed to shape, rather than respond to, family structure are unlikely to substantially reduce poverty, even in the long run.

Notwithstanding our assessment that the effects of policy on family formation are likely to be modest, it is noteworthy that even small changes in marriage patterns could produce substantial returns on fairly modest investments. It is too early to know whether recent efforts to promote healthy marriage will be successful; some policies to encourage marriage and, especially, reduce unplanned and teen pregnancy, may prove effective. Given the range of challenges faced by single parents, and especially by families formed by young, unmarried, and otherwise disadvantaged parents, developing appropriate contraception and relationship programs is a worthy focus for future research and evaluation, even while these programs are unlikely to substantially reduce poverty rates generally.

Conclusions of Investigation

The United States has adopted a work-focused antipoverty strategy that requires policies that support both parents' efforts to work and contribute to the economic support of their children. If resident parents, especially single mothers, are to meet their obligations as parents and workers, then they need supports including child care, workplace flexibility, and, for low earners, wage supplements (e.g., the EITC [Earned Income Tax Credit]) and subsidized health insurance. They also need an unemployment insurance system that recognizes that many workers who are the primary source of support for their families may also be the primary caregiver, necessitating part-time employment or temporarily leaving work to manage family responsibilities.

Enforcing the responsibility of nonresident fathers to provide for their children, and providing the supports necessary for them to work and meet their obligations, is another essential component of a work-based antipoverty strategy. Even disadvantaged fathers should be expected to support their children, and the support they pay should benefit their families, not offset government costs.

ARRA includes expanded funding for child care, a more generous EITC, and key expansions of the unemployment insurance program. It also temporarily restores a significant source of funding for child support enforcement. These changes are an important starting point for antipoverty policy supporting families, but most are time limited. While the recession highlighted the urgency of many of these programs, the needs they address are longstanding and require a sustained response.

> "Despite liberal howling and foot-stomping, not subsidizing illegitimacy led, like night into day, to less illegitimacy."

Welfare Reform Lowered Unwed Parenting Rates

Ann Coulter

Ann Coulter is a conservative author and syndicated columnist. In the following viewpoint, she asserts that the stimulus bill will roll back some of welfare reform's biggest accomplishments, especially lowering unwed parenting rates. Coulter argues that the stimulus bill will pay unwed mothers "to sit home doing nothing" and drive up the rate of children born into single-parent households. She also argues that the stimulus bill creates an untenable level of government bureaucracy and control, as well as adding nearly a trillion dollars to the national debt.

As you read, consider the following questions:

1. What does Coulter believe the stimulus bill will create?

2. What does Coulter state the 1996 welfare reform bill marked for the first time?

Ann Coulter, "Goodbye, America! It Was Fun While It Lasted," *Human Events*, February 11, 2009. Reproduced by permission.

3. According to the author, what will the stimulus bill
   mean that all bureaucrats at Health and Human Services
   do?

It's bad enough when illiterate jurors issue damages awards
in the billions of dollars because they don't grasp the difference between a million and a billion. Now it turns out the
Democrats don't know the difference between a million and a
trillion.

Why not make the "stimulus bill" a kazillion dollars?

All Americans who work for a living, or who plan to work
for a living sometime in the next century, are about to be
stuck with a trillion-dollar bill to fund yet more oppressive
government bureaucracies. Or as I call it, a trillion dollars and
change.

The stimulus bill isn't as bad as we had expected—it's
much worse. Instead of merely creating useless, make-work
jobs digging ditches—or "shovel-ready," in the Democrats' fe-
licitous phrase—the "stimulus" bill will create an endless army
of government bureaucrats aggressively intervening in our
lives. Instead of digging ditches, American taxpayers will be
digging our own graves.

There are hundreds of examples in the 800-page "stimulus" bill, but here are just two.

First, the welfare bureaucrats are coming back.

For half a century, the welfare establishment had the bright
idea to pay women to have children out of wedlock. Following
the iron laws of economics—subsidize something, you get
more of it; tax it, you get less of it—the number of children
being born out of wedlock skyrocketed.

The 1996 Welfare Reform bill marked the first time any
government entitlement had ever been rolled back. Despite
liberal howling and foot-stomping, not subsidizing illegitimacy led, like night into day, to less illegitimacy.

Stimulus Bill Takes Away Incentives to Marry

It's so diabolically simple: when you reward mothers financially for giving birth to illegitimate children and take away the welfare on which they've grown dependent when they marry—and when you consider that fatherlessness is the leading indicator of poverty, not because of pay inequality but because it takes a man and woman to effectively parent and provide for children—then you can see that Johnson's Welfare state was not a triumph for anyone other than the Democrats who keep the poor riled up with class envy and shuffled to the voting booths ... whenever needed.

Until Clinton's Welfare Reform—which encouraged the development of skills and work—there was no incentive for it to be otherwise ....

Barbara Curtis,
"Stimulus Bill Ends Welfare Reform—
Resurrecting the Poverty Cycle?"
MommyLife.net, February 20, 2009.

Welfare recipients got jobs, as the hard-core unemployables were coaxed away from their TV sets and into the workforce. For the first time in decades, the ever-increasing illegitimacy rate stopped spiraling upward.

As proof that that welfare reform was a smashing success, a few years later, Bill Clinton started claiming full credit for the bill.

Well, that's over. The stimulus bill goes a long way toward repealing the work requirement of the 1996 Republican Welfare Reform bill and rewards states that increase their welfare caseloads by paying unwed mothers to sit home doing nothing.

Second, bureaucrats at Health and Human Services will electronically collect every citizen's complete medical records and determine appropriate medical care.

Judging by the care that the State Department took with private visa records last year, that the Ohio government took with Joe the Plumber's government records, that the Pentagon took with Linda Tripp's employment records in 1998, and that the FBI took with thousands of top secret "raw" background files in President Clinton's first term, the bright side is: We'll finally be able to find out if Bill Clinton has syphilis—all thanks to the stimulus bill!

HHS bureaucrats will soon be empowered to overrule your doctor. Doctors who don't comply with the government's treatment protocols will be fined. That's right: Instead of your treatment being determined by your doctor, it will be settled on by some narcoleptic half-wit in Washington who couldn't get a job in the private sector.

And a brand-new set of bureaucrats in the newly created office of "National Coordinator of Health Information Technology" will be empowered to cut off treatments that merely prolong life. Sorry, Mom and Pop, Big Brother said it's time to go.

At every other workplace in the nation—even Wal-Mart!—workers are being laid off. But no one at any of the bloated government bureaucracies ever need fear receiving a pink slip. All 64,750 employees at the department of Health and Human Services are apparently absolutely crucial to the smooth functioning of the department.

With the stimulus bill, liberals plan to move unfirable government workers into every activity in America, where they will superintend all aspects of our lives.

Also, thanks to the stimulus bill, the private sector will gradually shrivel and die. According to the Congressional Budget Office, the cost of servicing the bill's nearly trillion-dollar debt will shrink the economy within a decade.

Robert Kennedy famously said: "There are those who look at things the way they are and ask, 'Why?' I dream of things that never were and ask, 'Why not?'"

The new liberal version is: *There are those who look at things and ask, "Why on earth should the government be paying for that?" I dream of things that never were funded by the government and ask, "Why not?"*

| "It is time the welfare [reform]-success
| fantasy be put to rest."

Welfare Reform Did Not Affect Unwed Parenting Rates

David R. Usher

David R. Usher is president of the American Coalition for Fathers and Children—Missouri Chapter. In the following viewpoint, he maintains that contrary to Ann Coulter's assertions, welfare reform was a failure because it did not reduce out-of-wedlock births or encourage two-parent families. Usher states that the proof is in the numbers: out-of-wedlock births are at record high levels and marriage rates are at a record low. He suggests that Republicans must push "marriage values" policies that address root social problems. Such policies, he asserts, will effectively assist women and men in a manner that also lessens government control over economic issues.

As you read, consider the following questions:

1. How much does Usher assert that illegitimacy rates have risen since 1996?

2. How many child support collections cases were there in 2006, according to Usher?

David R. Usher, "Coulter's Wrong on Illegitimacy Rates," WorldNetDaily.com, February 13, 2009. Reproduced by permission of WND.com Inc.

3. What was the total uncollected child support in 2006, as reported by Usher?

In her latest column, "Goodbye, America! It was fun while it lasted," Ann Coulter made a worrisome misrepresentation of illegitimacy and the Republican legacy of welfare reform:

> The 1996 Welfare Reform bill marked the first time any government entitlement had ever been rolled back. Despite liberal howling and foot-stomping, not subsidizing illegitimacy led, like night into day, to less illegitimacy.
>
> Welfare recipients got jobs, as the hard-core unemployables were coaxed away from their TV sets and into the workforce. For the first time in decades, the ever-increasing illegitimacy rate stopped spiraling upward.
>
> As proof that that welfare reform was a smashing success, a few years later, Bill Clinton started claiming full credit for the bill.

This (not uncommon) misunderstanding about welfare's success is destroying conservatives' ability to advance social policy thinking and develop a sorely needed winning political agenda.

It is time the welfare-success fantasy be put to rest.

Welfare Reform Failed

A brief history of the 1996 Welfare Reform legislation, followed by social data results, proves that welfare reform was not a success—particularly with respect to illegitimacy.

The 1996 federal welfare reform policy *goals* were based on findings contained in "Families First, the Report of the National Commission on America's Urban Families," issued in the last days of the H.W. Bush administration. The statement of findings of this document, adopted into welfare reform goals, was flawless. The goals of 1996 welfare reforms were to:

1. "provide assistance to needy families";

2. "prevent and reduce the incidence of out-of-wedlock births";

3. "encourage the formation and maintenance of two-parent families"; and

4. "end the dependence of needy parents on government benefits by promoting job preparation, work and marriage."

The 1996 welfare reforms were not successful because nothing in the legislation addressed items 2 and 3—the most important and politically positive elements of welfare reform goals.

Today, illegitimacy is at record levels—predominantly involving mature women aged 20 to 40. Since federal welfare reforms were enacted in 1996, illegitimacy has risen an astonishing 36.2 percent. Since 1960, when 5.3 percent of children were born out of wedlock, illegitimacy has skyrocketed 694 percent.

More Failures of Welfare Reform

Welfare reform has not improved marriage rates—which dived 22.7 percent since 1967. In fact, the marriage rate in 2005 was lower than the marriage rate during the 1932 Great Depression.

Poverty rates have improved since welfare reform was enacted in 1996. Between 1995 and 2005, poverty for single-female households fell 14.7 percent. But the record low for poverty was achieved in 1999 and 2000 and has been rising again at rate of .75 percent annually. This is primarily attributable to provisions forcing women to work (which had a corresponding negative impact on direct parenting of children and increase in child neglect rates).

Welfare reform brought about dramatic reductions in public welfare dependence. The number of families on welfare assistance declined 61.2 percent, from 4.54 million families in 1996 to 1.76 million families in December 2006.

The design of welfare reform essentially privatized welfare—substituting public welfare dependency for another major problem, tremendous amounts of uncollectible child support—yielding little actual net change in net welfare expenditures.

In 2006, there were 15.8 million child support collections cases covering 17.3 million children. Of these, 11.1 million child support cases were in arrears, and 6.8 million were not paying anything.

The child support arrearage for FY 1996 was only $8.1 billion. This exploded 369 percent to $29.9 billion for FY 2006. Total uncollected child support was $40 billion in 1996. This nearly doubled to $75.4 billion in 1999, to $83.9 billion in 2000, and reached a record $105.4 billion in 2006.

In the final analysis, welfare reform was more a failure than a success. This reality runs contrary to reports suggesting that welfare reform has been a success. The positive news about decreases in poverty and welfare caseloads does not survive the bad news about skyrocketing illegitimacy rates, decreased marriage rates, unrecoverable child support and child neglect.

The bad news reflected in other downstream consequences such as widespread health care coverage problems, retirement savings shortfalls, home-loan defaults, declining child well-being statistics and urban crime statistics indicates much work still needs to be done.

From an economic perspective, it is critical to understand that the bad news about the outcome of welfare reform, and the ensuing fiscal consequences, contributed significantly to the collapse of our financial systems.

Crafting Effective Welfare Policies

We must consider welfare reform an incomplete but necessary work in progress. The unstable state of welfare reform and our financial systems provides compelling reasons to complete what we set out to accomplish in 1996.

When we practice trickle-down social policy in concert with trickle-down economics, we can confidently predict a successful socioeconomic synergy the likes of which conservatives have not yet imagined—a victory for both social and economic conservatives.

Republican inactivity on social policy is a major reason why the GOP has been losing elections in droves since 1996. Illegitimacy immediately translates into votes for liberal politicians and a bigger welfare state. Now is the time to rebuild the Republican revolution, and to do it right this time.

I am working on "Marriage Values" policies and legislation in Missouri. The first legislation of the series should be introduced this session. I firmly believe that "Marriage Values" policies address root social problems in ways that are positive to women, men and taxpayers in ways that will render big government "solutions" as unnecessary and stupid as the caboose on a rusting steam-powered freight train.

| "We have a new division in America: those who pay a double fare, and those who forever ride free."

Food Stamps Have Contributed to an Overly Dependent Underclass

Patrick J. Buchanan

Patrick J. Buchanan is a conservative political commentator and author. In the following viewpoint, he contends that by allowing the food stamp program to expand, we have facilitated the dependence of millions of Americans on food stamps when they do not need them. Buchanan argues that the United States was more successful when it restricted government handouts like food stamps and instead required people to go out and work. He maintains that Americans of earlier generations survived much worse hardships than those facing today's Americans without the benefit of unemployment pay or welfare, and that their diligence and strong work ethic were a product of living in a society that required self-reliance.

Patrick J. Buchanan, "Food Stamp Nation," CNSNews.com, October 8, 2010. Reproduced by permission of Creators Syndicate.

As you read, consider the following questions:

1. How many Americans receive food stamps, according to Buchanan?

2. When was the Food Stamp Act signed according to Buchanan?

3. As of 2009, what does Buchanan cite as the cost to tax-payers of the US food stamp program?

"The lessons of history . . . show conclusively that continued dependence upon relief induces a spiritual and moral disintegration fundamentally destructive to the national fiber. To dole out relief in this way is to administer a narcotic, a subtle destroyer of the human spirit."

These searing words about Depression-era welfare are from Franklin Roosevelt's 1935 State of the Union Address. FDR feared this self-reliant people might come to depend permanently upon government for the necessities of their daily lives. Like narcotics, such a dependency would destroy the fiber and spirit of the nation.

What brings his words to mind is news that 41.8 million Americans are on food stamps, and the White House estimates 43 million will soon be getting food stamps every month.

A seventh of the nation cannot even feed itself.

If you would chart America's decline, this program is a good place to begin. As a harbinger of the Great Society to come, in early 1964, a Food Stamp Act was signed into law by LBJ appropriating $75 million for 350,000 individuals in 40 counties and three U.S. cities.

Yet, no one was starving. There had been no starvation since Jamestown, with such exceptions as the Donner Party caught in the Sierra Nevada in the winter of 1846–47, who took to eating their dead.

The Food Stamp Act became law half a decade after J.K. Galbraith in his best-seller had declared 1950s America to be the world's great Affluent Society.

Yet, when Richard Nixon took office, 3 million Americans were receiving food stamps at a cost of $270 million. Then CBS ran a program featuring a premature baby near death, and told us it was an infant starving to death in rich America. The nation demanded action, and Nixon acted.

By the time he left office in 1974, the food stamp program was feeding 16 million Americans at an annual cost of $4 billion.

Fast forward to 2009. The cost to taxpayers of the U.S. food stamp program hit $56 billion. The number of recipients and cost of the program exploded again last year.

Among the reasons is family disintegration. Forty percent of all children in America are now born out of wedlock. Among Hispanics, it is 51 percent. Among African-Americans, it is 71 percent.

Food stamps are feeding children abandoned by their own fathers. Taxpayers are taking up the slack for America's deadbeat dads.

Have food stamps made America a healthier nation?

Consider New York City, where 1.7 million people, one in every five in the city, relies on food stamps for daily sustenance. Obesity rates have soared. Forty percent of all the kids in city public schools from kindergarten through eighth grade are overweight or obese.

Among poor kids, whose families depend on food stamps, the percentages are far higher. Mothers of poor kids use food stamps to buy them sugar-heavy soda pop, candy and junk food.

Yet Mayor Michael Bloomberg's proposal to the Department of Agriculture that recipients not be allowed to use food stamps to buy sugar-rich soft drinks has run into resistance.

Food Stamps Are Outdated and Largely Unnecessary

Because of decades of economic growth, social conditions in America are far different today than they were when the food stamp program was created. Today, just 4 percent of U.S. households report even occasional hunger during the year. The main food-related health problem for children today is obesity, not hunger. Douglas Besharov of the American Enterprise Institute argues that poor Americans are generally suffering not from too little food, but from too much of the wrong kinds of food.

According to federal data, about two-thirds of American adults are "overweight" and about half of those are "obese." Obesity rates are actually higher for adults who are below the poverty level. Similarly, children below the poverty line are more likely to be overweight than other children. Despite these modern realities, food subsidy programs continue to support an out-of-date model of increasing the caloric intake of low-income Americans.

The food stamp program also sustains an out-of-date welfare concept of providing subsidies that are not conditioned on work status. The program contributes to long-term dependence on government and produces various social pathologies as side effects. Congress should end the food stamp program and allow the states to set their own policies.

Chris Edwards, "Food Subsidies," Downsizing the Federal Government, July 2009. www.downsizinggovernment.org.

"The world might be better . . . if people limited their purchases of sugared beverages," said George Hacker of the Center for Science in the Public Interest. "However, there are a great many ethical reasons to consider why one would not stigmatize people on food stamps."

The Department of Agriculture in 2004 denied a request by Minnesota that would have disallowed food stamp recipients from using them for junk food. To grant the request, said the department, would "perpetuate the myth" that food stamps users make poor shopping decisions.

But is that a myth or an inconvenient truth?

What a changed country we have become in our expectations of ourselves. A less affluent America survived a Depression and world war without anything like the 99 weeks of unemployment insurance, welfare payments, earned income tax credits, food stamps, rent supplements, day care, school lunches and Medicaid we have today.

Public or private charity were thought necessary, but were almost always to be temporary until a breadwinner could find work or a family could get back on its feet. The expectation was that almost everyone, with hard work and by keeping the nose to the grindstone, could make his or her own way in this free society. No more.

What we have accepted today is a vast permanent underclass of scores of millions who cannot cope and must be carried by the rest of society—fed, clothed, housed, tutored, medicated at taxpayer's expense for their entire lives. We have a new division in America: those who pay a double fare, and those who forever ride free.

We Americans are not only not the people our parents were, we are not the people we were. FDR was right about what would happen to the country if we did not get off the narcotic of welfare.

America has regrettably already undergone that "spiritual and moral disintegration, fundamentally destructive to the national fiber."

| "Some experts argue extending the food stamp program is beneficial for local economy."

Access to Food Stamps Is Essential for Needy Families

Jennifer DePaul

Jennifer DePaul is a producer and writer for the Fiscal Times. *In the following viewpoint, she examines the Barack Obama administration's plans to revise the requirements for food stamp benefits, broadening the availability of food stamps during the recent economic recession. DePaul notes that experts view the expanded program as a stimulus to local economies and the ethical thing to do for struggling families.*

As you read, consider the following questions:

1. According to the US Department of Agriculture as cited by DePaul, what is the lowest monthly cost of nutritious food for a family of four?

2. How much does DePaul state that the federal government spent on the food stamp program in 2010?

Jennifer DePaul, "Obama Administration Pushes to Expand Food Stamp Eligibility," *The Fiscal Times*, April 14, 2010. Reproduced by permission of The Fiscal Times Media Group, LLC.

3. How many Americans receive food stamps, according to USDA spokesperson Jean Daniel as quoted by DePaul?

A luveller Perkins, a single mother of four boys with an income barely above the poverty level, sought help in 2008 by applying for federal food stamps in Washington, D.C. But when social service workers reviewed her application, they found that her combined income and personal assets exceeded the limit by $50—and she was turned down.

The city's rules denied food stamps to applicants with monthly incomes in excess of $2,389 for a family of four with personal assets such as a car or furnishings worth more than $2,000. "It was disappointing," recalled Perkins, 36. "I toughed it out anyway," by keeping to a strict household budget and mastering the art of collecting coupons and buying food on sale.

Food Stamp Program Is Expanded

But now, Perkins's family and hundreds of other households in Washington with similar incomes and holdings could qualify for food stamp benefits averaging $234 a month. Last week [April 4–10, 2010], D.C. officials announced a major change in the income and assets limitations that will greatly expand the number of families that qualify for food stamps, now called the Supplemental Nutrition Assistance Program (SNAP). These new standards are part of a nationwide effort promoted by the [Barack] Obama administration to broaden the availability of food stamps amid one of the worst recessions in modern times.

The combination of 9.7 percent unemployment and high housing and food costs have forced many low-income families throughout the country to cut corners on food and forego nutritious meals. The lowest monthly cost of nutritious food for a family of four is $508, according to USDA figures, or about a fourth of the monthly income of a family of four living a little above the poverty level. The national average value of food stamp benefits per household is $275 per month, although it varies from state to state. Oregon offers one of the lowest average monthly checks per household at $229 while Alaska provides $430 per month.

The Obama initiative to expand the availability of food stamps has come with a substantial price tag. The federal government will spend an estimated $63.6 billion this year [2010] alone on the food stamp program—up from $34.6 billion in 2008, the last year of the Bush administration. The USDA funds 100 percent of the cost of food stamps and half of all state administrative costs.

More than 39 million Americans—or one in eight—receive food stamps, a historic high, according to Jean Daniel, a USDA spokesperson. Nearly a third of that total enrolled in the program during the past two years [2008–2010], since Obama took office. "This is a significant increase and is reflective of changes we've seen in economy," Daniel said. "The beauty of this program is that it was designed to expand or contract based on need."

Focusing on Working Families with Children

The move to open the doors to more individuals, known as broad-based categorical eligibility, eliminates an asset test and allows D.C. residents to earn up to 200 percent of the poverty level, or $3,675 per month for a family of four. The new rules also automatically accept families who may be on other forms of low-income assistance programs. These options aim to specifically help working families with children.

The District of Columbia, New Mexico and Alabama are the latest states and jurisdictions to implement the broader eligibility. Beginning with passage of the Welfare Reform Act in 1996, states were given the option to adopt broad-based categorical eligibility, but few did initially. Approximately 14

Cutting Food Stamp Benefits Hurts Single-Parent Families

Cutting the food stamp program will hurt women more than men. Look at who goes hungry in the U.S.: over a third of all single-female-headed households who have children are food insecure. No other household demographic is as likely to be going hungry. So, cut SNAP and who gets hurt? America's poorest women.

Raj Patel,
"Why We Shouldn't Cut Food Stamps to Pay for School Lunch,"
The Atlantic, November 23, 2010.

states signed on after the legislation passed. Since Obama took office, that number has doubled. According to the latest USDA statistics, 31 states are utilizing this tool to help people put food on the table.

"These expansion options have been growing in popularity and importance certainly as the recession has deepened and continued a way to get more SNAP benefits to more people," said Sheila Zedlewski, director of the Income and Benefits Policy Center at the Urban Institute, a liberal think tank.

Applications Are Streamlined

With many states facing budget crises and increased food stamp case loads, there is great appeal to adopt broad-based categorical eligibility. "Implementing the broad-based categorical eligibility helps states streamline the application process," said Dorothy Rosenbaum, hunger expert with the Center on Budget and Policy Priorities. States are cutting back staff while still trying to help people who are struggling during a recession, she said.

Some states have experienced marked surges in applications. Nevada has seen an 89 percent increase in household case loads from December 2007 to December 2009, the highest in the United States.

More states are conducting outreach, improving access to the programs, reducing the amounts of requirements for participants and adopting simplified policy options to reduce the administrative burden, according to USDA officials.

Some experts argue expanding the food stamp program is beneficial for local economy. For every dollar invested in SNAP over $1.84 goes back into the economy, said Melissa Boteach, manager of the Half in Ten Campaign at the Center for American Progress, a liberal think tank. Food stamps are one of the most effective stimulus programs out there, she said. "It's been one of the strongest elements of the social safety net," Boteach said. "It's worked. It's the right thing to do for struggling families and help economic stimulus."

Food stamps come in the form of an electronic debit card similar to an ATM card. Last week, Perkins paid a visit to the D.C. Department of Human Services and applied for a benefit check. "I hope it works out," Perkins said, who hopes to qualify for at least $200 per month. "That will take a great burden off of me financially. If it still doesn't work out for me I hope it works for other families behind me."

Periodical and Internet Sources Bibliography

The following articles have been selected to supplement the diverse views presented in this chapter.

Jennifer Bleyer	"Hipsters on Food Stamps," Salon.com, March 15, 2010.
Melinda Burns	"Welfare Reform Failing Poor Single Mothers," *Miller-McCune*, October 28, 2010.
Michelle Chen	"It's Time to Restore the Social Safety Net," *The Progressive*, June 16, 2010.
Francis X. Clines	"Running Against Food Stamps," *New York Times*, October 16, 2010.
Jason DeParle and Robert Gebeloff	"Food Stamp Use Soars, and Stigma Fades," *New York Times*, November 28, 2009.
Jason DeParle and Robert Gebeloff	"Living on Nothing but Food Stamps," *New York Times*, January 2, 2010.
Eric Dickson	"Who Wants Food Stamps?" Townhall.com, October 13, 2009.
Lisa Miller	"Divided We Eat," *Newsweek*, November 22, 2010.
Mark Niesse	"Food Stamp Usage Soars Among Working Families," *The Huffington Post*, October 22, 2010.
Ted Nugent	"Do Nothing, Get Nothing," *Washington Times*, January 28, 2011.
LaDonna Pavetti and Dorothy Rosenbaum	"Creating a Safety Net That Works When the Economy Doesn't," Urban Institute, April 2, 2010.

CHAPTER 4

What Are Some Alternatives and Improvements to the Welfare System?

Chapter Preface

In 2000 Michigan became the only state to impose mandatory random drug testing of welfare applicants and recipients. Lawmakers in the state were concerned with subsidizing drug addiction; it was essential, they maintained, that taxpayer money not be used to finance drug habits. Drug testing seemed to be a solution, because it would identify drug addicts and those intent on defrauding the system. The law immediately encountered resistance, however, as an opposition coalition formed to fight drug testing. The ACLU challenged the program as unconstitutional, maintaining that drug testing would violate the Fourth Amendment's protection against unreasonable searches. Groups including the Drug Policy Alliance, the American Public Health Association, the National Association of Social Workers, the National Council on Alcoholism and Drug Dependence, as well as other legal and health organizations submitted a brief elucidating their criticism of the law, arguing that Michigan's drug testing program would hurt the state's efforts to combat poverty and punish individuals and families.

In 2003 Michigan's mandatory drug testing program of welfare recipients was struck down when the US Court of Appeals for the Sixth Circuit upheld a lower court ruling finding the program to be unconstitutional. In her ruling on the case, *Marchwinski v. Howard*, US District Court Judge Victoria Roberts maintained that the state's rationale for testing welfare recipients "could be used for testing the parents of all children who received Medicaid, State Emergency Relief, educational grants or loans, public education or any other benefit from that State." She and other justices believed that allowing the random drug testing of welfare recipients could logically lead to policies whereby any large group of people receiving any kind of government benefit could be drug tested—a violation of the Fourth Amendment of the US Constitution.

Michigan was not the only state to consider implementation of a drug testing program for welfare recipients. Oregon tried, but found that drug testing was not very effective. New York and Maryland did cost-benefit analyses only to find that drug testing was too expensive and inefficient. Alabama discovered that job training programs were more effective than drug testing in moving people off welfare. Louisiana actually passed a drug testing law in 1997, but abandoned the idea when a task force concluded that a different monitoring system would be more successful and much less expensive than drug testing.

In fact, no other state has seriously attempted to implement a drug testing policy for welfare recipients. There are clear reasons for this: the courts have found them to be unconstitutional; state task forces have found them to be inefficient when compared to other methods; and moreover, they are widely considered to be too expensive and the money better spent on anti-poverty programs.

Yet many policymakers are still determined to find a way to establish drug testing for welfare applicants and recipients. In 2005 a House subcommittee amended the Personal Responsibility, Work, and Family Promotion Act to cut federal welfare funding to any state that did not drug test those applying for or receiving welfare benefits. Although it was never implemented, many lawmakers agreed with the aim of such provisions. In recent months, bills have been introduced in Kansas, Missouri, and West Virginia. Arizona has adopted a limited drug testing program. Many conservative politicians are pushing for more legislative challenges on the constitutionality of drug testing, hoping to overturn the earlier ruling in the Michigan case. Drug testing remains a common yet contentious issue in welfare policy discussions among lawmakers and policymakers.

Drug testing for welfare recipients is an issue explored in the following chapter, which examines alternatives and improvements to the current welfare system. Alternatives discussed include asset-building policies, job programs, the Earned Income Tax Credit, the Basic Income Guarantee, and a shift to private charity and pro-marriage policies.

"We not only need to educate the public about asset-based policies and their advantages, but also to gradually convert existing welfare programs to asset-based programs."

Incentives to Save Money Would Best Serve Low-Income Families

Sreya Sarkar

Sreya Sarkar is the director of the Asset Ownership Project at the Cascade Policy Institute. In the following viewpoint, she advocates the increasing popularity of asset-building policies as an alternative to traditional welfare programs, which provide money but do not encourage personal responsibility. Sarkar argues that asset-building accounts like Individual Development Accounts (IDAs) encourage low-income Americans to save money and build wealth, promoting asset-building skills and economic stability. She also adds that this approach will acquaint low-income families with the concept of saving, rather than simply spending and consuming.

Sreya Sarkar, "Wanted: Asset Accounts, Not Income Transfers," Cascade Policy Institute, August 6, 2008. Reproduced by permission of Cascade Policy Institute.

As you read, consider the following questions:

1. What two contradictory messages do low-income Americans hear from their government and anti-poverty organizations, according to Sarkar?

2. According to the author, what message do traditional public assistance programs aim at low-income individuals?

3. What does Sarkar view as the challenge to the growth of asset-building programs?

Low-income Americans hear two contradictory messages from government and "anti-poverty" organizations: "Save" and "Don't Save."

"Save" is the message from economists and many policymakers. They stress the importance of enabling low-income individuals to save and build wealth through work and personal responsibility, with help from government programs. Work and savings leads to the growth of personal assets, and assets are critical to long-term financial stability.

IDAs Encourage Saving

Michael Sherraden, one of the foremost American proponents of asset-based policies for the poor, commented in 2003 that the 21st century welfare state is in the midst of a transformation. Government handouts for consumption-related expenses should no longer be considered the "answer to reduce poverty."

Sherraden pioneered the concept of Individual Development Accounts (IDAS). Introduced more than a decade ago, IDAs are intended to encourage low-income Americans to save for constructive expenses like education, a first home or a car with which to be mobile enough to reach a higher-paying job. The goal of the IDA is to create a buffer against hardship and to promote both individual economic development and macroeconomic stability.

Sherraden considered asset-based policy proposals to be complementary to traditional welfare programs, not a replacement. Unfortunately, he failed to realize that in practice income-maintenance programs like welfare and asset-based policies like IDAs would conflict more than they would complement each other.

Finding an Alternative to Welfare

While the asset-building IDA movement says, "Save," the message from many government programs is, "Don't save." The existing array of public assistance aimed at low-income individuals (Temporary Assistance for Needy Families-TANF, food stamps, Medicaid, etc.) all say quite clearly, "Don't save," because eligibility for these "anti-poverty" programs involves limits on personal assets. Moreover, recipients are encouraged to spend out the monthly benefits, in order to avoid having the benefit levels cut back.

A growing body of evidence suggests that asset limits for welfare programs discourage low-income families from saving. Many low-income individuals avoid any kind of transaction with formal banking institutions, partly out of fear that owning a bank account would jeopardize their eligibility for public assistance. These government programs were originally conceived as short-term solutions to help struggling families and individuals, so they were not designed to facilitate long-term financial planning and independence.

Federal spending to assist low-income individuals is largely through programs like TANF, food stamps and housing assistance, programs unlikely to promote economic mobility and sometimes even inhibiting it, especially when it comes to intergenerational mobility.

These programs are consumption-oriented and essentially use-it-or-lose-it benefits. People using these programs have no incentive either to save or to leave the programs.

A recent New America Foundation publication entitled *The Assets Agenda* (2008) has tried to resolve this conflict between saving and not saving by suggesting reform of asset limits in all public assistance programs. It considers raising the asset limits in TANF and excluding certain asset holdings altogether, such as savings for retirement, automobile ownership and Earned Income Tax Credit (EITC) refunds.

But, is changing the asset limit for public assistance eligibility a permanent solution to avoid the conflict between saving and spending? Not really.

A Shifting Landscape

The American social policy landscape changed with the arrival of asset-based policies like Individual Retirement Accounts (IRAs), Health Savings Accounts (HSAs) and Individual Development Accounts (IDAs). These savings instruments are likely to continue to grow in popularity, possibly replacing New Deal-era social insurance programs (like Social Security and Unemployment Insurance) as the dominant form of 21st century social policy.

There is also a strong possibility that different types of asset accounts may be integrated into a single and flexible policy system of asset holdings belonging to individuals. For instance, each person might have a single account from birth with funds accumulating for education, homeownership, life and health insurance, some aspects of health care and retirement. In the United States, it seems likely that existing individual asset accounts (IRAs, HSAs, 401(k)s, Educational Savings Accounts, IDAs, etc.) might merge into one comprehensive system.

The challenge here is including the poor and the unbanked in this evolving system. If we stay on the present route, the poor will continue to be both excluded and confused because of the coexistence of two opposite policy paradigms (saving

History of IDAs

Individual development accounts are matched savings accounts that enable low-income families to save money for a particular financial goal, such as buying a home, paying for post-secondary education, or starting or expanding a small business. The framework for IDAs is widely believed to have emerged in the early 1990s through "asset-based" policy research that advocates asset-building programs to alleviate poverty.

Asset-based policy contends that traditional poverty programs that focus on income transfers, such as Temporary Assistance for Needy Families (TANF) payments or food stamp benefits, are necessary, but meet only short-term consumption needs. Asset-based policy proponents note that accumulating assets, such as contributing to a savings account or buying a home, over a longer time horizon creates a financial cushion for emergencies, which in turn generates social, behavioral, and psychological benefits. Armed with assets, an individual's options for emerging from poverty and entering the financial mainstream are greatly enhanced.

In 1993, Iowa was the first state to enact a law establishing IDAs. Today, 33 states (as well as Puerto Rico and the District of Columbia) have either laws or policies that govern the operations of IDAs. Of these states, 19 are currently operating programs that are supported by state funding. Approximately 540 community-based and -funded IDA programs operate across the United States including in the 17 states without IDA laws or policies.

FDIC Quarterly, *FDIC, 2011.*

and asset building versus "consuming and spending"). They will not fully participate in or utilize these promising asset-based policy proposals.

To include the poor we not only need to educate the public about asset-based policies and their advantages, but also to gradually convert existing welfare programs to asset-based programs. This could be done in TANF, Unemployment Insurance, Social Security and even public education—programs that collectively cost trillions of dollars without creating any direct assets for the recipients. This conversion would permanently resolve the savings conflict and would be a prudent public investment because it would increase the capabilities, engagement and productivity of all people and remove the work- and saving-related disincentives associated with the traditional welfare system in America.

> "A strategy to ensure that jobs reach the
> communities in which African-
> Americans live should include programs
> that jump-start job expansion where
> employment losses are heaviest."

Targeted Job Programs Could Reduce Poverty

Margaret Simms

*Margaret Simms is the director of the Low-Income Working
Families project at the Urban Institute. In the following viewpoint, she asserts that targeted job-training programs will be
needed to create jobs, improve job stability, and establish income
development in African American communities. Simms argues
that targeted jobs programs will be more effective than a more
general "just-generate-jobs" strategy because the latter has historically proved ineffective in the African American community.*

As you read, consider the following questions:

1. How many black Americans have been unemployed for
   every white American without a job for the past fifty
   years, according to Simms?

Margaret Simms, "Jobs Programs Must Be Targeted," *Milwaukee Journal Sentinel*, Janu-
ary 3, 2010. Reproduced by permission.

2. According to a Bureau of Labor Statistics report, how much more likely are African-American workers to have given up looking for work than whites?

3. What educational opportunities are cited by the author as a possible strategy for lowering unemployment?

America's 10% unemployment rate has overshadowed the plight of the chronically jobless and underemployed. Generating jobs is essential to sustaining the economic expansion that seems to be getting under way, but the initiatives adopted or proposed so far won't do much any time soon to help those who are habitually at the end of the job queue.

The tension between a "just-generate-jobs" strategy and targeted approaches shows up in the escalating battle between the Congressional Black Caucus and the White House. The caucus thinks its constituents—residents of 20 states plus the District of Columbia and the Virgin Islands—won't benefit from the ideas and programs on the table. Caucus members are mindful that many of the communities they represent—states that include more than 80% of the African-American population—missed out on the economic booms of the past decade and a half.

In Milwaukee and seven other Midwestern metropolitan areas represented by the caucus, job growth was only one-tenth that of the nation as a whole over the past 15 years. Half of the communities had fewer jobs in 2009 than in 1995, though the entire nation had 10% more. Even in the fast-growing South and West, about half the communities in the caucus fold fared worse than their counterparts, generating only 40% to 50% as many jobs as their Southern and Western sister metros during the high-growth 1995–2002 period.

African-Americans in this bloc of states and the District of Columbia will also wait longer for any jobs that do come to their communities. For the past half-century, there have been approximately two blacks unemployed for every white without a job. In November 2009, the African-American unemployment rate stood at 16%, compared with 9% for whites and 12% for Latinos.

The unemployment rate for African-Americans would have been even higher if many had not stopped looking for work because so few jobs were available. According to a new Bureau of Labor Statistics report, African-American workers nationally are more than twice as likely as whites to be in this category. When the economy was expanding in the 1980s, whites got jobs again about a year before black workers did. During the long expansionary period of the 1990s, the unemployment rate for adult African-American males was more than twice that of white adult males until the end of the decade.

So what's to keep the longstanding re-employment pattern from leaving African-Americans further behind as the recovery takes hold?

A strategy to ensure that jobs reach the communities in which African-Americans live should include programs that jump-start job expansion where employment losses are heaviest.

For example, Michigan had a 1% employment increase during October, but those 38,000 new jobs barely dented unemployment rolls, which had shot up to more than 700,000 people (not counting the many more who have given up looking for jobs). Perhaps the strategies being developed through the Recovery for Auto Communities program can be applied, modified or improved for use in the many communities nationwide now in distress.

Even strategies to create jobs in African-American communities alone won't improve job stability and upward mobility for African-Americans. Targeted job-training programs will be needed. Community organizations can be strong allies in developing programs and outreach initiatives that engage those trying to improve their employment prospects.

So far, much attention has been directed toward the community college system as an avenue for education and training, but alternatives are needed. Federal funds for work force training have been falling for the past two decades, at a time when jobs paying a family-sustaining wage increasingly require high-level skills.

Without these special initiatives, expect prolonged and deeper hardship. Black families have fewer employed workers to begin with and fewer assets to fall back on in hard times.

With some targeted help, these families could recover along with the rest of us.

> *"Private aid organizations have a better understanding that true charity starts with individuals making better life choices."*

Private Charity Should Replace Welfare

Michael Tanner and Tad DeHaven

Michael Tanner is an author and senior fellow at the Cato Institute and Tad DeHaven is a budget analyst for the Cato Institute. In the following viewpoint, they contend that private charities are more helpful to low-income families and individuals than government welfare programs. Tanner and DeHaven argue that private aid organizations understand that true charity starts with the understanding that people must develop self sufficiency and make wise life choices, and should not simply be handed a check every month. The authors maintain that private charities are better equipped to provide individualized aid and adjust eligibility standards to meet specific needs. In addition, they state that private charities are more efficient than government aid programs, so more of the donated funds can be used to benefit the recipients directly.

Michael Tanner and Tad DeHaven, "TANF and Federal Welfare," Cato Institute, September 2010. Reproduced by permission.

As you read, consider the following questions:

1. How much is federal spending on Temporary Assistance for Needy Families (TANF) per year, according to the authors?

2. According to Tanner and DeHaven, how many families receive TANF payments each month?

3. According to the authors, how much do Americans contribute to organized private charities every year?

The federal government funds a large range of subsidy programs for low-income Americans, from food stamps to Medicaid. This essay examines Temporary Assistance for Needy Families (TANF), which is a joint federal-state cash assistance program for low-income families with children. When most people think of "welfare," they are thinking of this program.

Since a major welfare reform in 1996, federal spending on TANF has been held fairly constant at somewhat less than $20 billion per year. The 2009 American Recovery and Reinvestment Act provided an additional $5 billion in federal funding over several years. About 1.8 million families receive TANF payments each month.

Before 1996, federal welfare was an open-ended entitlement that encouraged long-term dependency, and there was widespread agreement that it was a terrible failure. It neither reduced poverty nor helped the poor become self-sufficient. It encouraged out-of-wedlock births and weakened the work ethic. The pathologies it engendered were passed from generation to generation.

The welfare reforms of 1996 were dramatic, but the federal government still runs an array of welfare programs that are expensive and damaging. The federal government should phase-out its role in TANF and related welfare programs and leave low-income assistance programs to state governments, or better yet, the private sector.

Government welfare cannot provide the same flexibility and diversity as private charities. Private aid organizations have a better understanding that true charity starts with individuals making better life choices. Federal involvement in welfare has generated an expensive mess of paperwork and bureaucracy while doing little to solve the problem of long-term poverty.

Replacing Welfare with Private Charity

The 1996 welfare reforms were a step in the right direction, but much more needs to be done. The next step should be to transfer full responsibility for funding and administering welfare programs to the states. The states would have freedom to innovate with their low-income programs and would have strong incentives to reduce taxpayer costs and maximize work incentives.

The ultimate reform goal, however, should be to eliminate the entire system of low-income welfare for individuals who are able to work. That means eliminating not just TANF but also food stamps, subsidized housing, and other programs. Individuals unwilling to support themselves through the job market would have to rely on the support of family, church, community, or private charity.

What would happen to the poor if welfare were eliminated? Without the negative incentives created by the welfare state, fewer people would be poor. There would also likely be fewer children born into poverty. Studies suggest that women do make rational decisions about whether to have children, and thus a reduction in welfare benefits would reduce the likelihood of their becoming pregnant or having children out of wedlock.

In addition, some poor women who had children out of wedlock would put the children up for adoption. The government should encourage that by eliminating the present regula-

"Poverty USA," cartoon by Dave Granlund, PoliticalCartoons.com, September 17, 2010. Copyright © 2010 Dave Granlund and PoliticalCartoons.com. All rights reserved.

tory and bureaucratic barriers to adoption. Other unmarried women who gave birth would not be able to afford to live independently and they would have to live with their families or boyfriends. Some would choose to marry the fathers of their children.

Despite the positive social effects of ending government welfare, there will still be many people who make mistakes and find themselves in tough situations. Americans are an enormously generous people, and there is a vast amount of private charitable support available, especially for people truly in need.

Private charity is superior to government welfare for many reasons. Private charities are able to individualize their approaches to the circumstances of poor people. By contrast, government programs are usually designed in a one-size-fits-all manner that treats all recipients alike. Most government programs rely on the simple provision of cash or services without any attempt to differentiate between the needs of recipients.

The eligibility requirements for government welfare programs are arbitrary and cannot be changed to fit individual circumstances. Consequently, some people in genuine need do not receive assistance, while benefits often go to people who do not really need them. Surveys of people with low incomes generally indicate a higher level of satisfaction with private charities than with government welfare agencies.

Private charities also have a better record of actually delivering aid to recipients because they do not have as much administrative overhead, inefficiency, and waste as government programs. A lot of the money spent on federal and state social welfare programs never reaches recipients because it is consumed by fraud and bureaucracy.

Audits of TANF spending by the Health and Human Services' Inspector General have found huge levels of "improper payments," meaning errors, abuse, and fraud. In 2005, the state of New York had an improper TANF payment rate of 28 percent and Michigan had an improper payment rate of 40 percent. During 2006 and 2007, Ohio had an improper payment rate in TANF of 21 percent. There are similar high levels of waste in other states.

Another advantage of private charity is that aid is much more likely to be targeted to short-term emergency assistance, not long-term dependency. Private charity provides a safety net, not a way of life. Moreover, private charities may demand that the poor change their behavior in exchange for assistance, such as stopping drug abuse, looking for a job, or avoiding pregnancy. Private charities are more likely than government programs to offer counseling and one-on-one follow-up, rather than simply providing a check.

In sum, private charities typically require a different attitude on the part of recipients. They are required to consider the aid they receive not as an entitlement, but as a gift carrying reciprocal obligations. At the same time, private charities require that donors become directly involved in monitoring program performance.

Those who oppose replacing government welfare with private charity often argue that there will not be enough charitable giving to make up for the loss of government benefits. However, that assumes that private charity would simply recreate existing government programs. But the advantage of private and decentralized charity is that less expensive and more innovative ways of helping smaller groups of truly needy people would be developed.

If large amounts of aid continue to be needed, there is every reason to believe that charitable giving in the nation would increase in the absence of government welfare. In every area of society and the economy, we have seen that government expansion tends to "crowd out" private voluntary activities. So, in reverse, when the government shrinks, private activities would fill in the gaps.

A number of studies have demonstrated such a government crowd-out effect in low-income assistance. Charitable giving declined dramatically during the 1970s, as the Great Society programs of the 1960s were expanding. The decline in giving leveled out in the 1980s as welfare spending began to level out and the public was deluged with news stories about supposed cutbacks in federal programs. Then, after the passage of welfare reform in 1996, there was a large spike in private giving. Studies have also shown that when particular charities start receiving government funds, there is a decrease in private donations to those charities.

Americans are the most generous people on earth, contributing more than $300 billion a year to organized private charities. In addition, they volunteer more than 8 billion hours a year to charitable activities, with an estimated value of about $158 billion. Americans donate countless dollars and countless efforts toward providing informal help to families, neighbors, and others in need. There is every reason to believe that the elimination of government welfare would bring a very positive response both from recipients of government welfare and from Americans wanting to help those who are truly in need.

| "The United States could dramatically
reduce poverty—if it really wanted to."

A Comprehensive Anti-Poverty Policy Is an Alternative to Welfare

David R. Francis

David R. Francis is a columnist for the Christian Science Monitor. *In the following viewpoint, he suggests that it is time for a serious anti-poverty effort in the United States. Francis argues that such an effort would not be inordinately expensive and the economic and social benefits would be innumerable. He maintains that although the rate of poverty in the US has risen dramatically, especially among minority populations, the level of government aid to the poor has remained fairly static. Francis asserts that without a concerted effort to reduce poverty through programs such as universal health care, child care assistance, tax credit increases for the working poor, preschool education, and transitional help for parolees, the US economy and population will suffer devastating losses.*

David R. Francis, "The War on Poverty Is Winnable," *Christian Science Monitor*, April 2, 2007. Reproduced by permission.

As you read, consider the following questions:

1. What was the percentage of children in poverty in the United States in 2005, according to Francis?

2. According to the US Census Bureau, what was the overall poverty rate in the United States in 2005?

3. As stated in the viewpoint, what is considered the official poverty level in the United States?

The United States could dramatically reduce poverty—if it really wanted to. Instead, the number of American households in severe poverty (those with incomes less than half that of the official poverty level) has been growing, not shrinking.

"Poverty persists, not because we lack effective antipoverty policy options, but because we lack the political will to expand our policies," says Sheldon Danziger of the National Poverty Center, University of Michigan, Ann Arbor.

In 1964, President Lyndon Johnson launched the War on Poverty with the goal of lifting the "forgotten fifth" of the nation above the official poverty line. His economists predicted success by 1980 as the benefits of economic growth were shared over the years.

It didn't happen. The nature of the economy changed with globalization, high immigration, less unionization, and slower economic growth per capita. Instead, the income gap between the poor and the rich, especially the extremely rich, has greatly widened. This trend was recently acknowledged by President Bush, Secretary of the Treasury Henry Paulson Jr., and Federal Reserve Chairman Ben Bernanke.

"There's rising public concern about growing inequality," notes Peter Edelman, chair of a poverty task force at the Center for American Progress, a "progressive" think tank in Washington. His group will report later this month with recommendations for reducing poverty. "We know a lot more today [about] what to do," he says.

Nor would a serious antipoverty effort be inordinately expensive, he says. Its costs could be met by ending the "unnecessary and undeserved tax cuts" given the wealthiest Americans this decade, he claims. Winding down the Iraq war would also free funds to help the poor.

But will Washington step up such efforts? "There are no shakers and movers and lobbyists for the poor," says Neal Wolman, a social scientist at Manchester College, North Manchester, Ind.

Several observers speculate that a Democratic Congress and a Democratic president, should that occur, would be more likely to tackle poverty. "It takes presidential leadership," says Mr. Danziger. "It's not going to happen on its own."

Mr. Edelman and other poverty experts get some encouragement from the fact that Britain, under Prime Minister Tony Blair, has greatly reduced poverty by adapting or expanding various anti-poverty measures, some developed in the US. The proportion of British children living in poverty, for example, fell to 11 percent of the population in March 2005, down from 24 percent in 1998. Children's poverty in the US has been rising for the past few years to 17.8 percent in 2005.

The overall poverty rate in the US, reported by the Census Bureau last August, leveled off in 2005 at 12.6 percent, or 37 million. It had risen from 11.3 percent in 2000 with the onset of a mild recession.

Mr. Wolman is pleased by a decrease over the past 10 years in the high poverty rates of blacks and Hispanics. But nonwhites are still 2.6 times more likely to live in poverty than are whites. And children are 1.6 times more likely to be poor than adults are.

The rise in severe poverty has been noted by Dr. Steven Woolf, at the Department of Family Medicine, Virginia Commonwealth University, Richmond. In a paper in the American Journal of Preventive Medicine last October (joined by two other physicians), he found that the proportion of Americans

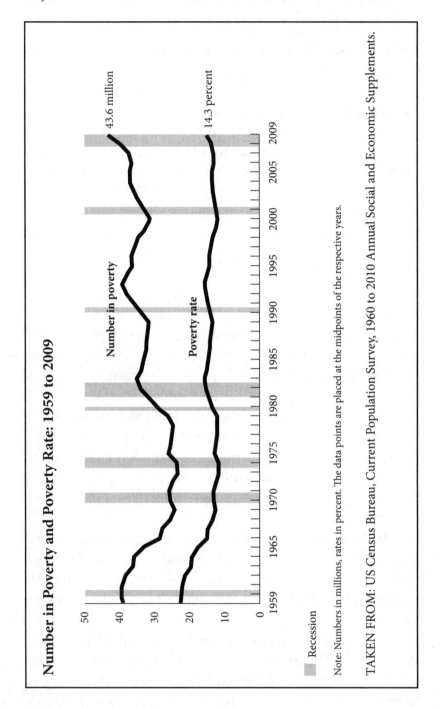

Number in Poverty and Poverty Rate: 1959 to 2009

Recession

Note: Numbers in millions, rates in percent. The data points are placed at the midpoints of the respective years.

TAKEN FROM: US Census Bureau, Current Population Survey, 1960 to 2010 Annual Social and Economic Supplements.

earning half or less of the official poverty level (which is $8,000 a year for an individual) grew by 20 percent from 2000 to 2004. In that time, the receipt of government aid (Medicaid, food stamps, tax credits, etc.) by the poor has not risen in real terms. The authors note that the risk of severe poverty is greater among blacks, Hispanics, and children.

Dr. Woolf's great concern with this trend is that it will worsen mortality rates and the incidence of disease among the poor. Social determinants like poverty and inadequate education do more damage to health than improving technology (new drugs, better medical devices) boost it, he says. The result of this trend could be even higher healthcare costs. "It will be very significant," he says.

A new study for the Center for American Progress offers an economic argument for reducing poverty, especially among children. It finds that costs associated with childhood poverty total about $500 billion a year, or nearly 4 percent of gross domestic product (GDP), the nation's total output of goods and services. Adults who grew up poor are more likely to be less productive and experience low earnings, engage in more crime, and suffer poorer health. Childhood poverty reduces national economic output each year by about 1.3 percent of GDP, raises the cost of crime 1.3 percent of GDP, and raises health costs by 1.2 percent of GDP.

An author of the study, Harry Holzer, an economist at Georgetown University in Washington, and other experts, list some antipoverty measures that should help: higher tax credits for the poor, health insurance coverage for all, more subsidized child care, more prekindergarten schooling, extra adjustment help for those leaving prison, and improved unemployment compensation.

> *"The design [of the Advance Earned In-*
> *come Tax Credit] is so flawed, it's prob-*
> *ably best to scrap it and start over."*

The Earned Income Tax Credit Should Be Reconfigured

Alan Berube

Alan Berube is the research director for the Brookings Metropoli-
tan Policy Program. In the following viewpoint, he maintains
that the US government must figure out a new and better way
to pay Earned Income Tax Credit (EITC) benefits to low-income
families. Berube notes that with new rules and regulations, tax-
payers are relying more and more on their annual tax refund,
which is paid as one lump sum instead of in monthly install-
ments. He concludes that this is an inefficient way to help strug-
gling families, and argues that changing regulations so that
families could receive payments throughout the year is crucial to
relieve some of their financial burdens.

As you read, consider the following questions:

1. What is the Advance EITC as described in the viewpoint?

Alan Berube, "While You Were Sleeping: Tinkering with the EITC," *New Republic*, August 10, 2010. Reproduced by permission.

2. How many eligible filers took advantage of Advance EITC according to the author?

3. What other industrialized countries with in-work tax credits pay them directly to eligible families on at least a monthly basis according to Berube?

Last week was an active one for America's stealth anti-poverty policy—the Earned Income Tax Credit (EITC)—though you'd be forgiven for not noticing. A couple of decisions, made with little fanfare, should have big implications for how low-income taxpayers receive the credit in the future.

The first development was a little disappointing. After a more than 30-year run, Congress seems poised to do away with the Advance EITC, to help offset a new round of federal aid to states. The Advance EITC is a little-used mechanism by which workers can get a portion of their expected EITC through their paycheck throughout the year. Under the program, employers can advance their workers up to $35 a week in credits, and then offset those payments against their payroll tax. But for a host of reasons, the Advance EITC never caught on with more than 1 percent of eligible filers, and the GAO found that the program suffered from a high degree of error. Our own research on the subject concludes that the design is so flawed, it's probably best to scrap it and start over.

Emphasis on "start over." With the expansion of the EITC and other refundable tax credits for families with children, more and more low-income filers are getting a significant amount of their annual earnings via a tax refund. It's time to ask whether we're really alleviating poverty, and "making work pay," to use President Clinton's phrase, when a low-earning mother with three children can receive upwards of half her annual income in a lump sum at tax time. These working families have pressing ongoing needs for food, shelter, and clothing, the bills for which don't come due just once a year. The fact that so many of these taxpayers use expensive "rapid

What Is the EITC?

The Earned Income Tax Credit or the EITC is a refundable federal income tax credit for low to moderate income working individuals and families. Congress originally approved the tax credit legislation in 1975 in part to offset the burden of social security taxes and to provide an incentive to work. When EITC exceeds the amount of taxes owed, it results in a tax refund to those who claim and qualify for the credit.

The Internal Revenue Service, 2011. www.irs.gov.

refund" loans to access these dollars just a few days before the IRS would deliver them testifies to the severe liquidity problems they face (more on that below).

The demise of the Advance EITC should obligate us to find a new and better way to pay the EITC periodically, throughout the year. Other industrialized countries with "in-work" tax credits—the U.K., Ireland, Australia, New Zealand—pay them directly to eligible families (not through employers) on at least a monthly basis. We've figured out how to do periodic tax payments, or may soon have to, to provide subsidies for health insurance, and for offsetting the impacts of climate change legislation on lower-income households. There are some tricky questions to contend with, including how to protect taxpayers whose circumstances change unexpectedly during the year from having to repay significant amounts. But we can strategically minimize the cost of those allowances, and the benefits of offering families real financial help throughout the year would far outweigh those costs.

Last week's other notable, more positive EITC development was IRS' decision to suspend availability of the "debt indicator" next tax filing season. This indicator, provided to tax professionals, enables preparers to identify whether or not the taxpayer's refund will be reduced via an offset for federal debts, such as prior-year taxes owed or student loan arrears. Sounds innocent enough, but the debt indicator essentially enables preparers to make those high-priced, essentially risk-free refund loans, most of them to low-income taxpayers who receive the EITC. Without it, the rapid-refund business will probably (hopefully) die a quick death.

That's a good thing for low-income taxpayers, though it won't necessarily do much to improve the dire financial conditions that drive some of these families to refund loans in the first place. With deficits as far as the eye can see, it's not clear that we'll be able to increase the EITC or other low-income credits significantly in the near future. In the meantime, getting more of the money to families throughout the year is a meaningful step we can take toward improving their financial security.

> *"Meeting one's own needs as well as your family's is more complex than just receiving a paycheck."*

A Basic Income Guarantee Can and Should Replace Welfare

Mark Radulich

Mark Radulich is a columnist for 411mania.com. In the following viewpoint, he argues that welfare reform was good in theory but has not worked as well as reformers thought it would. Radulich advocates the consideration of the Basic Income Guarantee (BIG), which requires the US government to provide a small monthly income to everyone, irrespective of their actual income, so that all Americans would have the security of knowing that they will always have enough money for basic expenses. He maintains that because it would eliminate the need for government oversight, the BIG is a truly conservative solution and should replace government welfare.

As you read, consider the following questions:

1. How does the author characterize conservative arguments about the welfare system?

Mark Radulich, "On Welfare and the Alternatives," 411mania.com, March 1, 2007. Reproduced by permission of the author, Mark Radulich, LCSW.

2. How many people rely on some form of public assistance, according to an Associated Press analysis?

3. What does Radulich think about conservative beliefs that all work is good work?

Poor people in society are a fact of life. So long as there is scarcity in resources, the ability for the powerful to command armies, and the human element of competitiveness, there will be poor people. But the definition of poverty ranges across the world. For example, poverty in the Bronx, NY is practically middle class compared to say poverty in any number of African nations.

In America, if you cannot find work or are laid off from your job, the government will send you a check. It won't be a lot, probably not a lot to live on but you won't starve either. And speaking of starving, the government will also send you money to buy food, will house you if you are homeless, provide health insurance if you haven't got any and will educate your children without asking you for a dollar.

None of the above are great solutions and anyone that has had experience with any of the above programs knows how woefully inadequate they are. The money the government sends you is not even close to enough to live on, the housing is usually substandard and in neighborhoods overwhelmed by crime, and the food/health programs are certified disasters, to say nothing of our public school systems in areas where there is also public housing.

Conservatives Misunderstand Poverty

Many conservatives will site some sort of moral failing as the reason why people are poor. These conservatives (many of whom are privileged) do not take into account systemic racism, misappropriations of government funds slated for development, industrial upheaval or just plain tragic bad luck. Many conservatives also seem to regard the welfare system as one in which people are paid to be slovenly or immoral and thus generations of this sort of behavior are encouraged thus expanding the welfare system.

They are not altogether wrong here but they are more wrong than right.

Welfare for a very long time was not means tested and in many cases it did encourage a breakdown of the family unit. If you worked at all but still couldn't pay your bills you were taken off the welfare roles so many people who could not find suitable work just stayed on welfare. In addition, women could receive more money per child they had and if there was no father present, thus creating a cycle of single-mother families, irresponsible parenting and general neglect of children in the poorest of areas.

During the NEWT [Newt Gingrich, Republican Speaker of the House, 1995–99] years of the [President Bill] Clinton administration, Congress and the president sought to reform welfare so that it would be means-tested and time limited thus forcing the cycle of degeneration to come to an end. However, a new article on the AP [Associated Press] is reporting that, 'The welfare state is bigger than ever despite a decade of policies designed to wean poor people from public aid. The number of families receiving cash benefits from welfare has plummeted since the government imposed time limits on the payments a decade ago. But other programs for the poor, including Medicaid, food stamps and disability benefits, are bursting with new enrollees.

The result, according to an Associated Press analysis: Nearly one in six people rely on some form of public assistance, a larger share than at any time since the government started measuring two decades ago.

Critics of the welfare overhaul say the numbers offer fresh evidence that few former recipients have become self-sufficient, even though millions have moved from welfare to work. They say the vast majority have been forced into low-paying jobs without benefits and few opportunities to advance."

All Work Is Not Equally Beneficial

The implication by those who sought to reform welfare by plading an emphasis on work is that all work is good work. Whether you're a cashier at Wal-Mart or the CEO of SLM Corp., it is theoretically all-equal in the eyes of the lord. Those of us living on planet earth know that this is simply conservative elitist balderdash. Manual labor or retail work may be respectable in lieu of not working or being a drug dealer but the reality is that besides earning a crap paycheck you'll have also earned the title, "working poor."

Ask anyone living in the North East or California if they can buy property or big-ticket items, decided markers of not living in poverty, on a retailers or Wal-Mart salary and when they are done laughing you'll get a hearty "no" for your troubles. The standard of living today in America is prohibitively so expensive that most of my friends who had decent jobs in their 20's still could not afford to live outside of their parent's homes. Those that could simply didn't want to as they didn't have to want to choose between relative comfort with little privacy and say, a cave next to Osama Bin Laden.

Now that's just us middle class folks—what about those closer to the poverty line that the article addresses? Once again, forcing people to work menial jobs with little pay also causes unintended and expensive consequences. These people, usually single women of white, black and Hispanic race, have to pay for daycare for their children since they are no longer afforded the luxury of being able to stay home and raise them. Daycare, let me tell you, is not all it's cracked up to be with regard to both practical and safety matters or the child's psychological development.

Programs That Resemble the Basic Income Guarantee

Alaska Permanent Fund	Basic Income (BI)	Basic Income Grant (BIG)
Citizen Dividends	Citizens' Dividend	Citizens' Income
Citizenship Income	Citizens' Wage	Daily Bread
Demogrant	Dividends for All	Guaranteed Annual Income (GAI)
Guaranteed Adequate Income (GAI)	Guaranteed Basic Income	Guaranteed Income (GI)
Guaranteed Minimum	Guaranteed Minimum Income	Income Guarantee
Minimum Income Guarantee	Minimum Income	Mincome
National Minimum	National Tax Rebate	Negative Income Tax (NIT)
Refundable Income Tax Credit	Rent Sharing	Share the Wealth
Social Credit	Social Dividend	Social Income
Social Wage	State Bonus	Territorial Dividend
Unconditional Basic Income (UBI)	Universal Allocation	Universal Basic Income (UBI)
Universal Benefit	Universal Grant	Universal Income Tax Credit

TAKEN FROM: "What Is the Basic Income Guarantee?," The US Basic Income Guarantee Network, www.usbig.net.

The fact of the matter is that making people work doesn't always solve the problem of self-sustainability. Meeting one's own needs as well as your family's is more complex than just receiving a paycheck. Inherent in the NEWT-Clintonian welfare reform bill is the belief that being a mom, with all of its subsequent duties is not worthy work. I dare any man reading this right now to tell their wife or their mother that what they do to keep the house running isn't worth spit. Go ahead, I'll wait.

The Basic Income Guarantee Solution

Now don't you feel sheepish? Getting back to conservative thought on this, if you want to decrease the size of government while making people self-sufficient and in doing so leaving the family unit intact, there is a rather simple solution that has been batted around since the Nixon administration.

The Basic Income Guarantee (BIG) is a government ensured guarantee that no one's income will fall below the level necessary to meet their most basic needs for any reason. As Bertrand Russell put it in 1918, "A certain small income, sufficient for necessities, should be secured for all, whether they work or not, and that a larger income should be given to those who are willing to engage in some work which the community recognizes as useful. On this basis we may build further." Thus, with BIG no one is destitute but everyone has the positive incentive to work. BIG is an efficient, effective, and equitable solution to poverty that promotes individual freedom and leaves the beneficial aspects of a market economy in place.

The term BIG is more specific than terms like income maintenance or income support, which refer to any kind of program designed to aid those with lower incomes. The Basic Income Guarantee differs from existing income maintenance programs in the United States and Canada in that it is both universal and has no work requirement. It is therefore, very simple and easy to administer. It helps the working poor, single parents, and the homeless, without placing anyone under the supervision of a caseworker ... The Basic Income gives every citizen a check for the full basic income every month, and taxes his or her earned income, so that nearly everyone both pays taxes and receives a basic income. Those with low incomes receive more in basic income than they pay in taxes and those with relatively high income pay more than they receive. The Negative Income Tax pays the full benefit only to those with no private income and phases out the benefit as people earn more private income, but private income is not taxed until the negative income tax is fully phased out. Thus, the Negative Income Tax avoids giving people checks and asking them to send checks back, but the Basic Income gives people the assurance that their check will be there every month if they have a sudden loss of income. Despite their differences both of these plans guarantee some basic minimum level of income and ensure that people who make more money privately will be financial better off than those who make less, and therefore both are forms of BIG.

I believe in dismantling the entire welfare system, Medicaid/care included and replacing it with the above BIG. This is the conservative solution without making judgments or convoluting it with man-managed bureaucracies as this would be the domain of the US Treasury department.

"The need for a more extensive economic safety net can be debated, but the need for a stronger moral safety net to protect women and children is indisputable."

Restoring a Culture of Marriage Will Reduce Poverty

Janice Shaw Crouse

Janice Shaw Crouse is an author and executive director of the Beverly LaHaye Institute of the Concerned Women for America. In the following viewpoint, she points out the increase of female-dominated households has increased the overall rate of poverty in the United States, noting that female-headed households tend to be poorer than two-parent homes. Crouse maintains that encouraging a change in women's attitudes toward premarital sex and restoring a culture of marriage will have a positive effect on poverty statistics.

As you read, consider the following questions:

1. What was the poverty rate in 2009, according to Crouse?

2. How much does Crouse indicate the number of female-headed households increased between 2003 to 2007?

Janice Shaw Crouse, "Sex, Poverty, and Recession," *Washington Times*, September 24, 2010. Reproduced by permission.

3. According to Crouse, how many million jobs were lost between 2007 to 2009?

The recent Brookings Institution briefing on the latest poverty estimates by the Census Bureau began with one of the panelists stating that there are "more poor persons today than ever." Her carefully worded statement ignores the fact that the rate of poverty has declined—the 2009 poverty rate of 14.3 was less than the 15.1 percent rate in 1993 or the 15.2 percent rate in 1983. The panelist also accurately claimed that the recovery from the recession of 2001 did little to lower poverty rates before they began to rise sharply from the effects of the current recession in 2008 and 2009. The Brookings panel set the stage for the subsequent Senate Finance Committee hearings, "Welfare Reform: A New Conversation on Women and Poverty," another event in the left's never-ending effort to promote increased welfare benefits.

The Brookings panel did not explore the economic and demographic circumstances that produce poverty, nor did it explain any of the reasons for the lack of progress in reducing poverty during the recovery from the 2001 recession. Note that from 2003 to 2007, the number of persons who were employed increased by 8.3 million, which lowered the unemployment rate from 6.0 percent to 4.6 percent. While this is not quite as large as the 9.3 million increase in the period from 1993 to 1997, it cannot be characterized as anemic.

At the same time that the economy was adding millions of jobs, however, cultural and demographic factors were at work to increase the number of poor. First, the number of persons living in female-headed households rose by 2.6 million and, second, the number of unrelated individuals living in the same household rose by 4.1 million from 2003 to 2007. It is precisely this demographic undertow that negated the effects of the recovery on the poverty rate.

Female-Dominated Households Have Increased

Given the financial difficulties unmarried mothers face in trying to raise a family—their family poverty rate is four to five times that of other families—it is no surprise that during the period from 2003 to 2007, three-quarters of the 1.4 million increase in the number of poor persons (which kept the poverty rate from declining) are accounted for by the growth in the number of poor persons in those female-headed households and the rest by growth in the number of poor unrelated individuals in the same household. It is worth noting that the poverty rate actually would have increased more had there not been a decrease of 240,000 in the number of poor persons living in all other types of families (i.e., those not having a female head of household).

With the economy mired in recession since 2007, the number of unemployed, plus those who have left the labor force has increased sharply, particularly among males. With the loss of more than 6 million jobs from 2007 to 2009, plus the continuing cultural and demographic undertow, the number of poor has jumped dramatically in all categories. The economy will recover eventually, but cultural and demographic changes make the challenge of combating poverty daunting because of the continuing growth in the high-poverty sectors of the population (i.e., unmarried mothers and unrelated individuals in the same household.

Women's Attitudes Toward Marriage Are to Blame

The question, then, is: What accounts for growth in the segment of the population that remains unmarried and economically isolated? David Gelernter provides an answer in his review of Martin Amis' "The Pregnant Widow" in the Weekly Standard. The change in women's attitudes about sex took the opening position from "No, unless I love you" to "Yes, unless I don't like you."

Economic Gains From Marriage

Married-couple families with children have much higher living standards and are less poor than other families. Although this observation tells us little about poverty's causes, research shows that additional marriages would likely reduce poverty, especially among low-income women. As shown in two recent simulation studies, marriages among unwed parents could reduce child poverty by as much as 25 percent. Among unwed mothers, marriage's positive effect on poverty rates appears greater among women at higher risk of being poor than among women at lower risk of being poor.

Robert I. Lerman,
"Should Government Promote Healthy Marriages?"
The Urban Institute, May 31, 2002.

The conventional wisdom these days is: "Nonmarital sexual relations are inevitable given that young people delay marriage in favor of getting an education and becoming established in a career. Besides, biology being what it is, men can hardly be expected to marry when female sexual partners are readily available without the accompanying responsibilities of marriage." A never-ending stream of novels and movies these days celebrate the unmarried pregnant women who choose to go it alone independent of the biological fathers. Hence, it is no surprise that nonmarital births now make up 40 percent of all births, which feeds the growth in the number of economically vulnerable single mothers.

This brings us back to the demand that the economic safety net be strengthened. Critics, like me, contend that this is the wrong approach. Resources should be focused on jobs programs that will bring the poor to the point of self-sufficiency; making poverty more tolerable in the welfare hammock only increases the problem. Given the growing body of research showing the adverse effects on children of growing up in fatherless homes plus the billions upon billions in taxpayer costs, the need for a more extensive economic safety net can be debated, but the need for a stronger moral safety net to protect women and children is indisputable.

> *"I'm not downing the welfare system; I just believe that it should be reserved for emergency situations, like people losing their jobs because of the economy and the disabled."*

Welfare Programs Should Include Mandatory Drug Testing

Ranee

Ranee is a writer and contributor to Helium. *In the following viewpoint, she expresses her strong support for mandatory drug testing of welfare recipients. Ranee argues that welfare should be reserved for emergency situations, not for drug addicts. She uses her own mother as a cautionary tale of a person who has abused both drugs and the welfare system, which she maintains has encouraged her mother's habits and has motivated others to engage in the same behavior.*

As you read, consider the following questions:

1. What option does the author believe a welfare recipient should have if he or she fails the drug test due to a prescribed drug?

Ranee, "Should Drug Tests Be Required of Welfare Recipients?" *Helium*, 2010. Reproduced by permission.

2. How does Ranee respond to Bill Piper's point that drug testing is an invasion of privacy?

3. How does Ranee state that her mother abused the welfare system?

This is one subject that gets me so heated. I totally agree with drug testing people on government assistance. I live in a town where there are so many people that are on welfare, some honestly do need it and some that could work but "play" the system and spend our tax dollars on dope. The same should apply to government testing as the workforce testing. If someone has to give a drug test for government assistance and fails due to a prescribed controlled drug, that doesn't mean that they won't receive assistance or that they will lose it. They simply have to prove that the drug is prescribed to them by a physician.

Bill Piper [Director of National Affairs of the Drug Policy Alliance] tries to debate the subject with Mike Bennett [US Senator from Colorado] on Fox News. Piper states that it is an invasion of privacy and would be humiliating for someone to have to admit that they are on Viagra or anti depressants. Honestly, if I were a man that lost my job and home and could not afford to feed my family, I would be more embarrassed to be on welfare than to reveal a certain prescription I'm on to the "stranger" giving me a drug test. If your kids are starving, that should NOT matter or even cross your mind! Bill Piper believes that drug testing recipients on welfare would be "too expensive" and risky for kids whose parents won't return to the DHS [Department of Human Services] office for extended funding due the fear of a drug test.

That's a good thing right? Wouldn't that encourage people to get clean to at least renew their food stamps? Piper believes that instead of testing we should just "expand access to treatment" (because you know an addict on welfare can't afford to go to rehab.) This guy is ridiculous. Welfare rehab? Is he being serious? That would cause taxes to go sky hi! He believes that people on drugs are able to work. They were once able to go to work until they went to work high and someone suspected it.... and they got DRUG TESTED and then FIRED! Someone should give Bill Piper a drug test! ... Okay seriously, if there is less people on welfare that could mean the taxes that aren't spent on jobless junkies go towards people who lost their jobs because of the economic recession or America's fast growing deficit that MY generation has to pay back.

Knowledge from Personal Experience

Growing up, my mother was a recipient who abused the welfare system. I remember having no heat or electricity and being so hungry it was painful. My siblings and I would fist fight over food. She would trade her food stamp card for various things like cash, cigarettes and an occasional joint. She just wouldn't help herself, and we were the kids that no one (DHS) cared about anyway and taxpaying working class people were forced to support her nasty habits. You can't help someone that won't help themselves.

She is still currently abusing the system today. She is getting loaded off my younger brother's social security check from his father who died of cancer almost a year ago and did not leave a will. As soon as she found out that his father died, she didn't call wondering where he was going to stay. She had not seen or heard from lil bro in years. Instead, she called my eldest brother leaving a voice mail laughing about his father's death and commenting on how she wasn't going to attend his funeral. When DHS found out that my mother still existed and contacted her in regards to him she was hesitant at first until she found out about the ssc checks and his father's belongings and he was forced to go live with her in her filthy cigarette-butt-infested rotting-maggot of a dump she calls home.

She made the comment to an u/k informant that "it was about time she got paid." My fourteen year old brother is not in school, and has not been in about a year. She claims she is homeschooling him just like she claimed to with me, but I know that he is just sitting in that musky old apartment wasting away at the hands of a person who doesn't pay her taxes, and abuses alcohol and drugs with our tax money.

Welfare Has a Role

I'm not downing the welfare system; I just believe that it should be reserved for emergency situations, like people losing their jobs because of the economy and the disabled. It shouldn't go to people like my mother who lack the incompetence to keep a job due to drug use. I am a hard working independent twenty two year old female student who doesn't make a whole lot of money at all, but you better believe that I work for every bit of what I make. I look at my pathetic little pay stub each pay period and I'm still thankful for my income. I don't give up and resort to drugs or try to intentionally get impregnated to receive welfare benefits. You would be surprised by how many young girls do that to receive income, but that's another subject

Weren't the Bill of Rights created to protect the rights of citizens ... so Piper is basically saying "you have the right to abuse drugs, and turn down a drug test because you have something to hide". Come on! it's just as easy as getting a physical in junior high to play a school sport, no one wants to get the physical because they're weird, but all the kids want to play ball. In the end the physical was for their own good. I know we can only control so much but it's our honest hard earned money, don't we have a RIGHT to know that it's going to a good cause?

> *"Given the high cost of treatment programs and the waiting lists for services in many areas, mandatory drug testing of all applicants or recipients of TANF benefits is a poor use of resources."*

Welfare Programs Should Not Include Mandatory Drug Testing

Matt Lewis and Elizabeth Kenefick

Matt Lewis and Elizabeth Kenefick are research assistants for the Workforce Development Team at the Center for Law and Social Policy (CLASP). In the following viewpoint, they maintain that mandatory drug testing programs for Temporary Assistance for Needy Families (TANF) recipients is an expensive and legally flawed proposition that is based on stereotypes of those receiving welfare. Lewis and Kenefick argue that policymakers should instead look to alternatives to mandatory drug testing, focusing on issues that help drug addicts, not those that put them and their families at risk during an economic downturn.

Matt Lewis and Elizabeth Kenefick, "Random Drug Testing of TANF Recipients is Costly, Ineffective, and Hurts Families," CLASP, February 3, 2011. Reproduced by permission.

As you read, consider the following questions:

1. According to estimates, what percentage of TANF recipients have a substance abuse problem?

2. What is the cost of catching a drug abuser through mandatory drug testing, according to the authors?

3. What is the only state that tried to impose mandatory drug testing on welfare recipients according to the viewpoint?

Mandatory drug testing for parents applying for or receiving assistance from the Temporary Assistance for Needy Families (TANF) program has been proposed repeatedly over the past few years. Legislators in at least 27 states have proposed suspicionless drug testing with some even extending it to recipients of other public benefits as well, such as unemployment insurance, medical assistance and food assistance. At the federal level, Senator David Vitter (R-LA) has offered bills and amendments multiple times to impose mandatory drug testing on TANF recipients and deny them eligibility if they failed a second test after treatment. The most recent is *The Drug Free Families Act of 2011* (S 83). Last summer, Senator Orrin Hatch (R-UT) proposed mandatory drug testing for TANF and unemployment insurance recipients.

Proposals for mandatory drug testing of TANF recipients are based on stereotypes and not evidence. Proponents often claim that drug testing will save money; however, this is based on a false assumption that many applicants will be denied benefits. Random testing is a costly, flawed and inefficient way of identifying recipients in need of treatment. Better alternatives exist and are already being implemented to address drug abuse among TANF beneficiaries and ultimately reduce their barriers to work. Moreover, universal random drug testing may well be unconstitutional. In 2003, Michigan's drug testing program was struck down as a violation of the Fourth

Amendment's protection against searches without reasonable cause. Finally, because sanctions for noncompliance put vulnerable children at risk, state and federal policymakers should not enact more barriers to a safety net program that protects low-income children and families, especially during an historic economic downturn and decline in the labor market.

Drug Testing is Based on Stereotypes

Research finds little evidence that drug use and/or abuse is particularly prevalent among TANF beneficiaries. Although recent data is limited, and definitions and populations vary, studies have put the portion of the TANF recipient population with a substance abuse disorder at anywhere between five and 27 percent, and those reporting illicit drug use around 20 percent or less.

In 1996, the National Institute of Alcohol Abuse and Alcoholism found that "proportions of welfare recipients using, abusing, or dependent on alcohol or illicit drugs are consistent with proportions of both the adult U.S. population and adults who do not receive welfare." Furthermore, Michigan, the only state to have imposed random drug testing on TANF beneficiaries, found that only 10 percent of recipients tested positive for illicit drugs, with 3 percent testing positive for "hard" drugs, such as cocaine. These rates are consistent with its general population. While other studies show that TANF recipients are somewhat more likely to have tried illicit drugs or have substance abuse disorders than the general population, the fact remains that a large majority of recipients do not use drugs.

For a small group of TANF recipients, substance abuse is a significant barrier to employment. One survey of TANF directors, found that they considered substance abuse the third most significant barrier to work for recipients. States do already have policies to identify and treat such individuals. Substance abuse problems tend to co-occur with mental health and social problems. TANF recipients with substance abuse problems have been shown to have a high incidence of mental and social disorders. Many individuals turn to drugs and alcohol as a way to try to control symptoms of mental illness.

Drug Testing is Expensive and Inefficient

Random, widespread drug testing is an inefficient use of taxpayer money as multiple states have determined. It is costly to administer, especially when precautions are taken to prevent false results, and is not cost-effective for identifying true cases of substance abuse. Testing should be limited to cases where agencies have good cause to believe that a client may be using drugs, and where the client has acknowledged use and agreed to participate in a treatment program.

Administrative costs associated with drug testing are significant, and the tests themselves each cost anywhere from $35–76. These costs are increased by the need to repeat tests to confirm results and avoid false positives. Therefore, in order to provide due process protections against false positives, many states such as Idaho and Utah would have to require confirmation of results, meaning human service agencies may have to conduct repeat tests of split samples before imposing sanctions. It is not cost effective to test all applicants or participants, regardless of whether they show any indications of drug use. Since few substance abusers are identified in tests, but many are tested, the cost of catching a drug abuser may run between $20,000 and $77,000 per person, as businesses and government employers have found when they have done testing.

Furthermore, chemical drug tests have more significant shortcomings as they cannot identify alcohol or prescription drug abuse, but rather only the specific chemicals for which samples are tested. More importantly, they cannot distinguish between occasional substance users and substance abusers. While drug abuse problems pose a barrier to work and economic advancement, drug use alone does not appear to have a significant impact on employment outcomes and government service usage rates. In a study of Florida TANF recipients, individuals who tested positively for drug use had earnings and were employed at nearly the same level as individuals who had tested negatively. In another study, drug use was as prevalent among employed TANF recipients as among the unemployed. This is also true of the general population, as most drug users have full-time employment.

Many advocates for drug testing all recipients imply that state human services agencies are doing nothing to identify substance abuse among recipients, but proven alternatives to chemical tests have been developed and are already being implemented. More than half of states responding to a survey in 2002 reported that they were screening for drug abuse. Most states use a "screen-and-refer" method of detection and treatment promotion. Typically, a paper-and-pencil test is administered. One such test, the Substance Abuse Subtle Screening Inventory (SASSI), has an accuracy rate of between 89–97 percent, can distinguish between drug users and abusers, and can detect alcohol abuse. The Oklahoma Department of Human Services found that a questionnaire they administered identified 94 out of 100 drug abusers. Paper tests and caseworker observation also have the benefit of being less intrusive and costly than drug testing when there is not yet a reasonable basis to require a drug test.

Still, research has shown that this method of detection can be improved. Many of the workers administering drug screening are inexperienced. Eighty percent of states in a 2002 survey reported that they assign this task to welfare caseworkers, as opposed to mental health specialists, and nearly three-quarters reported that they provided less than eight hours of training for workers. Some states have developed more involved alternatives to detect drug abuse. Evaluating an intensive case management (ICM) referral system in New Jersey, re-

The Case of Louisiana

Louisiana passed a law in 1997 requiring drug testing for welfare recipients. However, a task force set up to implement the law found more limited drug testing of individuals identified by a questionnaire to be more cost-effective than mandatory drug testing.

"Drug Testing of a Public Assistance Recipients as a Condition of Eligibility," ACLU, April 8, 2008.

searchers found that TANF recipients with a substance use disorder who participated in the ICM system were more likely to abstain from drugs and find employment than those assigned to a screen-and-refer program.

Many states do impose drug testing requirements on TANF recipients who have been identified as at high risk of substance abuse. This may include participants who have agreed to participate in treatment in lieu of other work activities. Some states also require clean drug tests as a condition of restoring benefits to recipients who have been convicted of drug-related felonies.

Drug Testing May Be Unconstitutional

Only one state, Michigan, has ever made all adult TANF recipients submit to random drug tests. In *Marchwinski v. Howard*, the ACLU challenged Michigan's across-the-board testing and the district court ruled in September 2000 that it violated the recipients Fourth Amendment rights against unreasonable searches. The U.S. Court of Appeals for the Sixth Circuit reversed the decision, but then withdrew the reversal in 2003 after rehearing the case and splitting the vote.

Random searches are only justified if they meet a high legal standard. In general, individualized suspicion is necessary to perform a search. States may and do impose drug testing requirements on individuals who have been identified as substance abusers, or as a condition of reinstating benefits for an individual convicted of a drug-related felony. However, simply receiving cash assistance is not a basis for suspicion of substance use and the state must have some reason to believe that a particular individual may be using drugs.

Sanctions Put Vulnerable Children at Risk

Many of the proposals call for denying assistance to anyone who fails a drug test. Imposing additional sanctions on welfare recipients will have negative impacts on children. Welfare sanctions and benefit decreases have been shown to increase the risk that children will be hospitalized and face food insecurity. Because TANF benefits are so low (less than 1/3 the poverty level in the median state), children suffer even when only the "adult portion" of the benefit is eliminated. Without these benefits, families may be unable to meet children's core basic needs, such as housing and clothing. The impact on children may be even greater now because of few job openings and family budgets already stretched due to the recession.

Sanctions may also interfere with the treatment process by deterring people from reporting an abuse issue and seeking treatment. Also, treatment and recovery are not a one-time event. Many people require a series of treatment sessions and relapse rates are high. If TANF recipients are sanctioned, they may lose access to treatment programs that may take time and repeated efforts to show results.

No study has shown that denying assistance facilitates substance abuse treatment. On the contrary, the most effective drug treatment programs show that TANF recipients require additional support. Transportation, housing and child care support help parents overcome barriers to successful program completion. Denying access to benefits will increase barriers to economic advancement and family well-being.

Additional Funding and Comprehensive Treatment Are Needed

Drug treatment is an efficient use of taxpayer money. A national study of treatment programs serving women found significant employment gains, a modest rise in income, and a modest decline in the number receiving public benefits. The benefits of treating TANF recipients in California, according to one study, exceeded the costs by more than two and one half times. States are seeing the benefits of treatment and investing in programs. About 60 percent of states in a 2002 survey indicated that they had invested TANF funds in alcohol and drug treatment in FY2002. California, for instance, has put $50 million a year in treatment, as the percentage of CALWORKS parents receiving substance abuse treatment tripled over the last decade.

Several comprehensive treatment options have also shown positive results. Drug abuse problems tend to co-occur with mental health and social problems, and low-income women with children face significant logistical barriers to completing treatment programs. More comprehensive treatment programs meet transportation, housing and child care needs, as well as provide employment counseling and mental health services. One comprehensive approach to treatment in New York and North Carolina, called CASAWORKS for Families showed positive results. Other states, including Oregon and Arizona, have set up a cross-agency collaborative to deal with the different dimensions of substance abuse. In Louisiana, a demonstration project with an intensive screening, referral, and treatment system slightly raised employment levels and significantly improved wages.

Drug Testing Is a Poor Use of Resources

Given the high cost of treatment programs and the waiting lists for services in many areas, mandatory drug testing of all applicants or recipients of TANF benefits is a poor use of resources. In a time of tight state budgets, it is perverse to spend limited funds in pursuit of the small number of substance abusers who are not identified through screening processes, rather than on providing actual services. Despite the persistence of proposals to impose drug testing at the state and federal levels, these proposals have consistently been rejected because the data do not support the money-saving claims. In the late 1990s, New York, Maryland, Iowa, and Louisiana considered drug testing, but decided it was more cost-effective to use questionnaires and observational methods to detect substance abuse problems. Last year, Idaho's Department of Health and Welfare was commissioned to study the financial sustainability of requiring tests and is in the process of reporting that it would not save any money.

Moreover, if identified drug users are sanctioned and not provided with treatment services and basic cash assistance, these parents are less able to adequately care for their children. Thus, what might appear to be savings in TANF will actually result in increased costs in child welfare and decreased overall child wellbeing.

Periodical and Internet Sources Bibliography

The following articles have been selected to supplement the diverse views presented in this chapter.

Frank Cerabino	"Hypocritical Scott Is Reverse Robin Hood," *Palm Beach Post*, August 10, 2010.
Marian Wright Edelman	"The Threat of Persistent Poverty," *Huffington Post*, November 16, 2010.
Alan Greenblatt	"Should Welfare Recipients Get Drug Testing?" *NPR*, March 31, 2010.
Ron Haskins	"The Rise of the Bottom Fifth: How to Build on the Gains of Welfare Reform," *Washington Post*, May 29, 2007.
Clifford M. Johnson, Amy Rynell, and Melissa Young	"Publicly Funded Jobs: An Essential Strategy for Reducing Poverty and Economic Distress Throughout the Business Cycle," Urban Institute, April 2, 2010.
Alec MacGillis	"The Poverty of Political Talk," *The American Prospect*, August 26, 2009.
Jennifer Marshall	"Fight Poverty—Restore Marriage," The Heritage Foundation, October 8, 2010.
Signe-Mary McKernan and Caroline Ratcliffe	"Asset Building for Today's Stability and Tomorrow's Security," Urban Institute, December 1, 2009.
Don McNay	"The Season for Tax Refund Ripoffs," *Huffington Post*, January 30, 2011.
Phillip S. Smith	"Drug Tests for Unemployment Checks? Just Cheap Political Theater," *AlterNet*, March 22, 2009.
Nathan Tabor	"Drug Testing for Welfare Recipients," *Renew America*, April 23, 2007.

For Further Discussion

Chapter 1

1. The first five viewpoints in this chapter analyze the efficacy of welfare reform in the United States. After reading all of them, which do you believe is the most persuasive? How do you feel welfare reform has performed?

2. Welfare programs attract controversy. Anthony DiMaggio asserts that such programs combat poverty and prove to be beneficial to those who need them. Others counter by arguing that welfare perpetuates dependency and does not make a significant dent in the rate of poverty in America. Do you think welfare is a positive program for the poor? Back up your opinion with information found in the viewpoints.

Chapter 2

1. Israel Ortega contends that the Stimulus Bill, passed in response to the recent economic downturn, has essentially reversed the 1996 welfare reforms. Sharon Parrott disagrees with that assessment. Read both viewpoints. Do you think welfare reform has been reversed by the provisions of the Stimulus Bill?

2. Should the TANF Emergency Fund be renewed and expanded to help those affected by the economic downturn? Read viewpoints written by Rachel Sheffield and Christine L. Owens and George Wentworth to inform your answer.

3. Do you think that Congress should provide incentives for promoting marriage? After reading the viewpoint by Chuck Donovan and Robert Rector, enumerate the advantages and disadvantages of such incentives.

4. Do you think there needs to be a job program for the unemployed who have left welfare? After reading the viewpoint by Anthony J. Mallon and Guy V.G. Stevens, enumerate the advantages and disadvantages of such a program.

Chapter 3

1. In his viewpoint, Ron Haskins maintains that pro-marriage policies are essential in the fight to reduce welfare. Maria Cancian, Daniel R. Meyer, and Deborah Reed argue that pro-marriage policies do not help families and do not significantly impact the need for welfare programs. Which view do you think has more merit? Use information from the viewpoints to support your opinion.

2. Has welfare reform lowered the number of unwed parents? Use arguments made by Anne Coulter or David R. Usher to inform your answer.

3. The economic downturn has led to an explosion in the use of food stamps. Patrick J. Buchanan argues against this trend, pointing out that food stamps perpetuate dependency and should therefore be restricted to only the most needy cases. Jennifer DePaul maintains that access to food stamps is essential during the recent economic crisis. In your opinion, are food stamps a key tool in helping those affected by the recession? How accessible should food stamp programs be?

Chapter 4

1. Viewpoints 1 through 7 in this chapter examine some alternatives to the current welfare system in the United States. Which ones do you think hold promise and why?

2. After reading the first seven viewpoints in this chapter, what alternatives to the welfare system discussed seem to be insufficient, unrealistic, or unworkable? Support your opinion by using information from the viewpoints.

3. In recent years there has been an increased call for mandatory drug testing for welfare recipients. Ranee argues that testing is essential to eliminate fraud in the program. Matt Lewis and Elizabeth Kenefick maintain that mandatory drug testing is too costly, inefficient and has a negative effect on families. In your opinion, should drug testing be instituted? Why or why not?

Organizations to Contact

The editors have compiled the following list of organizations concerned with the issues debated in this book. The descriptions are derived from materials provided by the organizations. All have publications or information available for interested readers. The list was compiled on the date of publication of the present volume; the information provided here may change. Be aware that many organizations take several weeks or longer to respond to inquiries, so allow as much time as possible.

American Public Human Services Association (APHSA)
1133 19th Street NW, Suite 400, Washington, DC 20036
(202) 682-0100 • Fax: (202) 289-6555
Website: www.aphsa.org

The American Public Human Services Associations (APHSA) is a nonprofit organization that was founded in 1930 to improve the lives of US families by supporting state and local agencies, educating policymakers, and developing innovative and effective solutions to issues such as child care, child welfare, and welfare. The organization also hosts conferences and seminars to disseminate the latest human services information, practices, and policies. APHSA publishes two e-newsletters: *NAPCWA Weekly Update* and *This Week in Washington*, which explores relevant human services issues. The APHSA website also posts recent news, commentary, and policy updates.

Children's Defense Fund (CDF)
25 E Street NW, Washington, DC 20001
(800) 231-1200
E-mail: cdfinfo@childrensdefense.org
Website: www.childrensdefense.org

The Children's Defense Fund (CDF) is a national nonprofit children's advocacy organization that works to help children by championing policies and programs that lift kids out of poverty, protect them from abuse and neglect, create educational opportunities, and ensure equal access to quality healthcare services. The CDF monthly e-newsletter offers updates on these efforts and explores topical issues and news. The CDF website hosts a weekly column by Marian Wright Edelman, the CDF president and lifelong activist, as well as audio clips, photos, and video.

Coalition on Human Needs (CHN)

1120 Connecticut Ave. NW, Suite 312, Washington, DC   20036
(202) 223-2532 • Fax: (202) 223-2538
E-mail: infor@chn.org
Website: chn.org

The Coalition on Human Needs (CHN) is a network of national organizations that advocate for well-considered policies to help low-income families and individuals, the elderly, and the disabled. CHN hosts meetings, forums, and working groups of their member organizations to communicate information, find consensus, and develop and implement innovative strategies on public policy issues. CHN publishes the *Human Needs Report*, a monthly e-newsletter that explores national policy issues affecting low-income and vulnerable populations. In addition, the CHN website provides access to reports, analyses, studies, and other publications focused on poverty, housing, and welfare.

Institute for Research on Poverty (IRP)

1180 Observatory Drive, 3412 Social Science Bldg.
Madison, WI   53706
(608) 262-6358 • Fax: (608) 265-3119
E-mail: djohnson@ssc.wisc.edu
Website: www.irp.wisc.edu

The Institute for Research on Poverty (IRP) is a center at the University of Wisconsin-Madison that is focused on compiling research on "the causes and consequences of poverty and social inequality in the United States." It is one of the three Area Poverty Research Centers sponsored by the US Department of

Health and Human Services (HHS). IRP publishes *Focus*, a newsletter that covers poverty-related research, events, and news; and *Fast Focus*, an e-newsletter that provides information on IRP research and events between issues of *Focus*. The IRP website features links to the latest discussion papers, research studies, and special reports. It also offers abstracts on the latest books published by IRP.

MRDC
16 E. 34th Street, 19th Floor, New York, NY   10016
(212) 532-3200 • Fax: (212) 684-0832
E-mail: information@mrdc.org
Website: www.mrdc.org

MRDC is a nonprofit, nonpartisan education and social research organization focused on improving and developing anti-poverty programs. Established in 1974, MRDC evaluates current programs, diagnoses strengths and weaknesses, develops a plan to improve them, and informs policymakers and stakeholders. MRDC's specialty is welfare-to-work programs. The MRDC website offers research presentations, policy briefs, in-depth studies, how-to-guides, fact sheets, and a variety of video clips and presentations. The Newsroom section of the website lists recent news and updates on MRDC research and events.

National Coalition for the Homeless (NCH)
2201 P Street NW, Washington, DC   20037
(202) 462-4822 • Fax: (202) 462-4823
E-mail: info@nationalhomeless.org
Website: www.nationalhomeless.org

The National Coalition for the Homeless (NCH) is a national network of homelessness activists, community-based and faith-based service providers, and policymakers determined to end homelessness. NCH also addresses the needs of the homeless population, and advocates for services and policies that will provide immediate help to those on the street. The organization publishes a monthly e-newsletter, as well as manuals, reports, factsheets, and in-depth studies. The NCH website also features the latest news on homelessness efforts, legislation and policy, and NCH events and educational programs.

National Governors Association (NGA)
444 N. Capitol Street, Suite 267, Washington, DC 20001
(202) 624-5300 • Fax: (202) 624-5313
E-mail: webmaster@nga.org
Website: www.nga.org

The National Governors Association (NGA) is a bipartisan group of US governors that disseminates policy reforms and innovations, shares effective practices and policy ideas, and networks to improve state services and leadership. NGA provides management and technical assistance to new and experienced governors, as well as other services to help governors improve their performance. The NGA website features press releases, issue papers, speeches, video, photos, reports, member bios, and issue summaries. The NGA Center for Best Practices' Economic, Human Services & Workforce (EHSW) Division focuses on the most effective practices and policy options on topical issues such as economic development and innovation, employment services, research and development policies, and human services for children, youth, low-income families, and people with disabilities.

National Education Association (NEA)
1201 16th Street NW, Washington, DC 20036
(202) 833-4000 • Fax: (202) 822-7974
Website: www.nea.org

Founded in 1857, the National Education Association (NEA) is the largest labor union in the United States. The NEA represents more than 3.2 million public school teachers, school employees, college instructors and staffers, and retired educators. The association's mission is "to advocate for education professionals and to unite our members and the nation to fulfill the promise of public education to prepare every student to succeed in a diverse and interdependent world." The NEA's activities range from raising money for scholarship programs to developing training and leadership programs for teachers to lobbying for appropriate levels of school funding from local, state, and federal governments. The NEA Today is a website that offers stories on education topics, as well as access to the *NEA Today* magazine. The NEA also publishes *Thought & Action*, a journal focused on education theory; *Tomorrow's Teachers*, a resource for teachers; and *Higher Education Advocate*, a bimonthly newsletter that explores issues important in higher education.

Urban Institute
2100 M Street NW, Washington, DC   20037
(202) 833-7200
Website: www.urban.org

The Urban Institute is a nonpartisan, independent think tank focused on gathering data, evaluating programs, providing technical assistance, and educating US policymakers and citizens on social and economic issues. The organization's ultimate mission is to facilitate and support effective social and economic policy as well as sound urban governance. The Urban Institute offers a range of e-newsletters on its website, such as the *Urban Institute Update*, which provides updates on events, publications, and programs; and the *Low-Income Working Families Newsletter*, covering new findings by the Low-Income Working Families Project. The organization also publishes a number of books, which can be ordered through the publications catalog on the Urban Institute's website. Also featured is pertinent commentary, audio of past events, press releases, video, testimony from experts, and fact sheets on poverty and welfare.

US Department of Health and Human Services (HHS)
200 Independence SW, Washington, DC   20201
(877) 696-6775
Website: www.hhs.gov

The Department of Health and Human Services (HHS) is the US agency tasked with providing essential human services.

The HHS oversees the Administration for Children and Families (ACF), a department that manages and develops programs that for welfare, child welfare, child support enforcement, foster care, adoption assistance, and child abuse. ACF is focused on empowering families and individuals to achieve economic independence; providing services to the poor, the neglected, refugees, and the disabled; and fostering strong, robust, and safe communities. The HHS and ACF websites offer information on the latest programs and events, fact sheets, reports, manuals, and issue briefs as well as other publications shedding light on the department and its efforts to help US families and individuals.

Bibliography of Books

Peter Alcock and   *Welfare Theory and Development.*
Martin Powell,   Thousand Oaks, Calif.: SAGE
eds.   Publications, 2010.

Phillip A.   *Temporary Assistance for Needy*
Bernard, ed.   *Families: TANF and the Recession.*
                     Hauppauge, NY: Nova Science
                     Publishers, 2010.

Martin Binder   *Elements of an Evolutionary Theory of*
                     Welfare: Assessing Welfare when
                     Preferences Change. New York:
                     Routledge, 2010.

Richard K.   *U.S. Social Welfare Reform.* New York:
Caputo   Springer, 2011.

Marisa Chappell   *The War on Welfare: Family, Poverty,*
                     and Politics in Modern America.
                     Philadelphia: University of
                     Pennsylvania Press, 2010.

Jane L. Collins   *Both Hands Tied: Welfare Reform and*
and Victoria   *the Race to the Bottom in the*
Mayer   *Low-Wage Labor Market.* Chicago:
                     University of Chicago Press, 2010.

Lew Daly   *God's Economy: Faith-Based Initiatives*
                     and the Caring State. Chicago:
                     University of Chicago Press, 2009.

Kevin Farnsworth   *Social Policy in Challenging Times:*
and Zoe Irving,   *Economic Crisis and Welfare Systems.*
eds.   Bristol, England: Policy Press, 2011.

Miguel Ferguson   *Caught in the Storm: Navigating Policy and Practice in the Welfare Reform Era.* Chicago: Lyceum Books, 2010.

Tony Fitzpatrick   *Welfare Theory: An Introduction to Theoretical Debates in Social Policy.* 2nd. rev. ed. New York: Palgrave Macmillan, 2011.

Michael E. Fix, ed.   *Immigrants and Welfare: The Impact of Welfare Reform on America's Newcomers.* New York: Russell Sage Foundation, 2009.

Daniel P. Glitterman   *Boosting Paychecks: The Politics of Supporting America's Working Poor.* Washington, DC: Brookings Institution Press, 2010.

David P. Levine   *Welfare, Right, and the State: A Framework for Thinking.* New York: Routledge, 2008.

Betty Reid Mandell, ed.   *The Crisis of Caregiving: Social Welfare Policy in the United States.* New York: Palgrave Macmillan, 2010.

Sandra Morgan, Joan Acker, and Jill Weigt   *Stretched Thin: Poor Families, Welfare Work, and Welfare Reform.* Ithaca: Cornell University Press, 2010.

Herbert Obinger, et al.   *Transformations of the Welfare State: Small States, Big Lessons.* Oxford: Oxford University Press, 2010.

Frank Ridzi   *Selling Welfare Reform: Work-First and the New Common Sense of Employment.* New York: New York University Press, 2009.

Karen Seccombe   *"So You Think I Drive a Cadillac?": Welfare Recipients' Perspectives on the System and Its Reform.* Boston: Allyn & Bacon, 2007.

Kristin S. Seefeldt   *Working after Welfare: How Women Balance Jobs and Family in the Wake of Welfare Reform.* Kalamazoo, Mich.: W.E. Upjohn Institute for Employment Research, 2008.

Barbara Vis   *Politics of Risk-Taking: Welfare State Reform in Advanced Democracies.* Amsterdam: Amsterdam University Press, 2010.

William Voegeli   *Never Enough: America's Limitless Welfare State.* New York: Encounter Books, 2010.

Lisa C. Welch   *What Welfare Reform Says About the United States of America: Values, Government Bureaucracy, and the Expansion of the Working Poor.* Lewiston, NY: Edwin Mellen Press, 2009.

James P. Ziliak   *Welfare Reform and Its Long-Term Consequences for America's Poor.* New York: Cambridge University Press, 2009.

Index